COLLECTED PRAYERS FOR ADVENT, CHRISTMAS AND EPIPHANY

FOR PUBLIC WORSHIP

NICK FAWCETT

kevin mayhew

kevin
mayhew

First published in Great Britain in 2015 by Kevin Mayhew Ltd
Buxhall, Stowmarket, Suffolk IP14 3BW
Tel: +44 (0) 1449 737978 Fax: +44 (0) 1449 737834
E-mail: info@kevinmayhew.com

www.kevinmayhew.com

9 8 7 6 5 4 3 2 1 0

ISBN 978 1 84867 785 2
Catalogue No. 1501481

Cover design by Rob Mortonson
© Images used under licence from Shutterstock Inc.
Typeset by Richard Weaver

Printed and bound in Great Britain

Contents

About the author

Brought up in Southend-on-Sea, Essex, Nick Fawcett trained for the Baptist ministry at Bristol and Oxford, before serving churches in Lancashire and Cheltenham. He subsequently spent three years as a chaplain with the Christian movement Toc H, before focusing on writing and editing, which he continues with today, despite wrestling with cancer. He lives with his wife, Deborah, and two children – Samuel and Kate – in Wellington, Somerset, worshipping at the local Anglican church. A keen walker, he delights in the beauty of the Somerset and Devon countryside around his home, his numerous books owing much to the inspiration he unfailingly finds there.

Introduction

'Hi Nick. Do you have something among your many prayers on the subject of Mary . . . of Joseph . . . of Advent expectation . . . of the shepherds . . . of the magi . . .?' So I could continue. I've lost count of the number of phone calls, letters or emails I've received along just such lines from friends, colleagues or readers seeking inspiration concerning a particular theme. And it's always good being able to help if I possibly can. The trouble sometimes, though, is knowing where to look. Yes, I think, I'm sure I wrote something on that somewhere, but where was it exactly? With numerous prayer and study books now in print, it's difficult to remember in which of them a particular prayer appears, so I end up thumbing through one after another before I finally track it down. What I really needed, I decided, was all the prayers of a particular type organised in one place, and so was born the series of which this book is the second, alongside collected intercessions and collected prayers for Lent, Holy Week and Easter.

Here you will find in a single volume all of the prayers for Advent, Christmas and Epiphany I've written over the years, many of them revised and adapted for public worship through the addition of congregational responses. They are arranged under the themes of Approach, Praise, Confession, Thanksgiving, Petition and Intercession, with the addition of closing and reflective prayers, and a short section for Christingle. The aim is to offer an easy-to-use resource that will offer help and inspiration to all those entrusted with leading public prayer during this special time of year.

If this compilation helps you to articulate more fully something of the wonder of these much-loved seasons, then it will more than have served its purpose.

Nick Fawcett

ADVENT

First week of Advent

Approach

1

Lord Jesus Christ,
we have come to worship you in this glad season of Advent,
a season of expectation,
of celebration,
and, above all, of preparation.
We come now, because we want to be ready –
ready to give thanks for your coming,
to recognise the ways you come to us now,
and to welcome you when you come again.
Open our hearts as we worship you,
so that all we share may give us a deeper understanding of this season
and a fuller experience of your love.
Amen.

Praise

2

Loving God,
we rejoice in this season of good news and goodwill;
we celebrate once more the birth of your Son,
our Saviour Jesus Christ,
the Prince of Peace,
the Lord of lords,
the Word made flesh,
and we praise you for the assurance of his final triumph.
For your coming through him,
and promise to come again,
Lord, we worship you.

We rejoice at your coming among us through Jesus,
bearing our flesh and blood,
living our life and sharing our humanity,
entering our world,
and walking our earth.
For your coming through him,
and promise to come again,
Lord, we worship you.

We rejoice at your suffering and dying among us,
your victory over death,
triumph over evil,
and promise that the kingdom will come.
For your coming through him,
and promise to come again,
Lord, we worship you.

We rejoice at the wonder of this season,
its message of love and forgiveness,
its promise of peace and justice,
and the gift of life everlasting of which it speaks.
For your coming through him,
and promise to come again,
Lord, we worship you.

Loving God,
we rejoice again in this season of good news and goodwill,
and we look forward to that day when the Jesus of Bethlehem will be the
Lord of all.
For your coming through him,
and promise to come again,
Lord, we worship you.
Amen.

3
Loving God,
we praise you again for this season of Advent,
this time of preparation, thanksgiving, challenge and reflection.
Open our hearts to all you would say now,
and help us to listen.

We praise you that in fulfilment of your eternal purpose
you came to our world in Christ,
revealing the extent of your love,
showing us the way to life,
allowing us to know you for ourselves.
Open our hearts to all you would say now,
and help us to listen.

We praise you that you came again in Christ to his disciples after his
resurrection,
bringing joy where there had been sorrow,
hope where there had been despair,
and faith where there had been doubt.
Open our hearts to all you would say now,
and help us to listen.

We praise you that through your Holy Spirit you make Christ real to us
each day,
filling us with his power,
his peace,
and his love.
Open our hearts to all you would say now,
and help us to listen.

And we praise you for the promise that Christ will come again
to establish his kingdom,
to begin a new era,
to bring us and all your people life everlasting.
Open our hearts to all you would say now,
and help us to listen.
Amen.

Confession

4
Loving God,
forgive us that so easily we lose sight of the message of Advent,
allowing its wonder to be swamped by our busy preparations for Christmas,
by concerns that are so often unimportant,
by our carelessness and disobedience in discipleship.
Lord, hear us,
graciously hear us.

Forgive us that we forget your promises,
frustrate your Spirit,
and lose sight of your love.
Lord, hear us,
graciously hear us.

Meet with us, we pray, through this time of worship,
through your living Word,
through the fellowship we share,
and through the risen Christ,
so that we may truly celebrate the advent of your Son,
and be equipped to serve him better.
Lord, hear us,
graciously hear us.
Amen.

5
Lord,
we pray often that your will may be done
and your kingdom come,
but we rarely stop to consider what that involves.
For the weakness of our discipleship,
forgive us.

It's something we ask of *you*,
expecting *you* to accomplish it,
you to do the spadework,
forgetting that you need people like *us* to be your hands and feet,
your agents within the world,
proclaiming the gospel,
sharing your love,
offering our service.
For the weakness of our discipleship,
forgive us.

Forgive us, Lord, for abdicating our share of the responsibility.
Forgive us for seeing the kingdom solely as some future paradise,
and so ignoring the hell some endure today.
For the weakness of our discipleship,
forgive us.

Teach us to reach out in the name of Christ,
and through our life and witness to contribute something meaningful to
your purpose,
so that a glimpse of heaven may shine through on earth,
to your praise and glory.
For the weakness of our discipleship,
forgive us.
Amen.

Thanksgiving

6

Loving God,
we thank you for this glad time of year,
this Advent season that reminds us of so much,
and that reveals so wonderfully the extent of your love.
For your coming and coming again in Christ,
we thank you.

Thank you for the challenge this season brings to look back
and remember the birth of your Son,
light into our darkness;
to look forward and anticipate his coming again,
as he returns to establish your kingdom and rule in your name;
and, above all, to reflect on the present,
examining our lives,
searching our hearts,
exploring your word,
renewing our faith
and recognising more fully that Jesus is with us each moment of every day,
now and always.
For your coming and coming again in Christ,
we thank you.

Loving God,
you came to our world in humility,
born of Mary in a stable.
You will come once more in glory,
through the risen and ascended Christ.
You are with us now even as we speak,
here through your Holy Spirit making Jesus real!
We praise you for the great truth of Advent.
For your coming and coming again in Christ,
we thank you.
Amen.

Petition

7

Lord of all,
you tell us to wait and pray for that time when Christ will come again
to establish his kingdom;
that time when your purpose will be fulfilled
and your name made known and worshipped on all the earth!
You challenge us to live in the light of that promise –
help us to respond.

Teach us never to lose sight of your purpose,
never to stop believing that you are at work,
never to lose confidence in your kingdom.
Teach us that, as Christ came, so he will come again.
You challenge us to live in the light of that promise –
help us to respond.

But teach us also not to waste the present,
nor to place all our hope in the future,
nor to imagine that you are unconcerned for us and your world now!
Teach us to recognise that Christ is with us always,
by our side to the end of time.
You challenge us to live in the light of that promise –
help us to respond.

Help us to live and work for you always,
rightly and responsibly enjoying your many gifts,
and seeking to do your will and follow your ways.
Help us to live each day as though Christ were about to return,
until that day when he appears in glory
and you are all in all.
You challenge us to live in the light of that promise –
help us to respond.
Amen.

8

Loving God,
you have told us to look forward to a time when your kingdom will come
and your will be done –
a time when there will be an end to sin and evil,
suffering and sorrow;

when all your people will live together in peace and harmony;
when Christ will come again in glory.
Light of the world,
come to us now, we pray.

Loving God,
forgive us that so often we have lost our sense of expectation,
content simply to get by,
settling for the way things are,
failing to believe you can change our lives or transform the world.
Light of the world,
come to us now, we pray.

Forgive us that we have been too full of our own expectations,
believing we know all there is to know,
pushing you into little boxes we have made for you,
presuming your thoughts and your ways are the same as ours.
Light of the world,
come to us now, we pray.

Forgive us that our expectations have been limited,
tied down by our imperfect vision,
restricted to our narrow horizons,
shaped by looking at life from an immediate rather than eternal perspective.
Light of the world,
come to us now, we pray.

Loving God,
help us through all this season of Advent has to say to us,
to gain a new sense of expectation
and new confidence in the future;
Help us to be open to all you would do among us,
and to gladly respond.
Help us to catch sight of the wonder of your coming in Christ,
so that we may be ready to greet him when he comes again.
Light of the world,
come to us now, we pray.
Amen.

9
Eternal God,
Ruler over space and time,
Lord of history,
before all, in all, and beyond all,

we worship and acknowledge you,
recognising afresh that your ways are not our ways,
nor your thoughts our thoughts.
Lord, in your mercy,
hear our prayer.

Forgive us for sometimes losing sight of that fact,
presuming we know better than you,
even expecting you to do our bidding
rather than us doing yours.
Lord, in your mercy,
hear our prayer.

Teach us that you are beyond our greatest imagining,
higher than our loftiest dreams;
and that you do things in your own way and time,
expecting us to wait patiently,
trusting in your wisdom and purpose.
Lord, in your mercy,
hear our prayer.

When our prayers do not seem to be answered,
our ambitions remain unfulfilled,
and our faith appears to be in vain,
save us from premature judgements.
Lord, in your mercy,
hear our prayer.

Teach us that it is often at such times as these –
especially at such times as these –
that we need to believe in you and your timing.
Give us grace to accept our part in your scheme of things,
and to leave the rest to you.
Lord, in your mercy,
hear our prayer.
Amen.

10
Lord Jesus Christ,
as we prepare once more to celebrate your coming into the world,
help us to reflect more fully on what it means
and what it cost you.
You surrendered everything;
gladly we offer our lives back to you.

Teach us to rejoice in the light you have shone into the world –
the light of your word,
your truth,
your love,
your life –
and to walk in it each day.
You surrendered everything;
gladly we offer our lives back to you.

Help us also to recognise that you endured the darkness of hatred and evil,
of suffering and death,
to ensure that this light would not be extinguished
but would continue to shine for ever.
You surrendered everything;
gladly we offer our lives back to you.

Remind us that Advent speaks not only of your birth in a stable
but also of your death on a cross,
and that it is this that has made possible new birth for all.
You surrendered everything;
gladly we offer our lives back to you.
Amen.

11
Mighty God,
you promise that, for those who love you,
all things will work together for good,
but it's not always easy to believe that assurance in the traumas and turmoil
of life.
Reach out, O God,
and restore our faith.

We face so much that seems to deny your love
and frustrate your will,
our world being scarred by suffering and sorrow,
evil and injustice,
that leaves few of us untouched.
Reach out, O God,
and restore our faith.

All too often hopes are dashed and dreams broken by the icy blast of reality,
such that, though we still speak of your purpose for our lives,
it becomes hard to see how your hand might be at work,
weaving the tangled and broken threads of our daily experience
into a rich a meaningful tapestry.
Reach out, O God,
and restore our faith.

Teach us to see beyond the here and now to your eternity,
beyond present pain to future blessing,
beyond current despair to promised jubilation.
Reach out, O God,
and restore our faith.

Help us to recognise that though life now may make no sense,
all will one day become clear;
that though evil seems triumphant,
good will finally prevail.
Reach out, O God,
and restore our faith.
Amen.

12
Lord Jesus Christ,
as you came once,
so you will come again to establish your kingdom
and to fulfil the purpose of the One who sent you.
Help us to learn from your first coming
and to remember that, despite the long years of expectation
and the desire of so many to see you,
few found room for you when you finally came.
Save us, then, from complacency,
and teach us to live each day to your glory,
happy at each moment to stand in your presence
and ready to welcome you on the day of your return.
Amen.

13
Lord Jesus Christ,
though we speak of your coming again,
your return to establish your kingdom,
it's hard to anticipate it meaningfully,
and part of us doesn't want to,
for you've given so much here and now that's good,
and it would seem wrong to overlook this life through dwelling on the next.
Yet don't let us lose altogether our sense of expectation;
the conviction that one day your will shall be done –
sorrow overcome,
evils righted,
love triumphant,
death itself destroyed.
Help us to celebrate today in the light of your tomorrow.
Amen.

14
Loving God,
open our eyes to see you,
our ears to hear you,
our hearts to love you
and our lives to serve you.
So may we share in the work of your kingdom
and the fulfilment of your will,
to the glory of your name.
Amen.

15
Gracious God,
we praise you that you came to our world in Christ,
fulfilling your promise of old,
vindicating the long-held expectations of your people.
We praise you that you came again to the apostles in the risen Christ,
appearing when you were least expected
bringing new hope and immeasurable joy.
We praise you for the promise that you will come again in Christ
to establish your kingdom
and to give life to all your people.
Teach us to live every moment of every day
in the light of the eternal tomorrow you hold in store for us
and for all your people,
through Jesus Christ our Lord.
Amen.

16
Lord Jesus,
we like to think we're ready for your return –
to serve you,
respond to your call
and welcome you when you come again –
but we wonder sometimes whether we're actually anywhere near it,
for the faith and vision that once coursed within us so easily drains away,
our energy and enthusiasm dissipated,
leaving behind a discipleship that flatters to deceive.
Come, and fill us afresh,
so that we may live and work for you.
Amen.

17

Lord Jesus Christ,
we have no claim on your goodness,
no right to expect your blessing,
for, compared to you, we are nothing –
weak,
stubborn,
foolish.
Yet you invite us not just to know you
but to make you known,
not just to love you
but to be loved in turn,
not just to enter your kingdom
but to help build it now.
Thank you for that awesome grace,
so undeserved
yet so freely given.
Amen.

18

Gracious God,
it's hard sometimes to keep faith that your kingdom will come,
for so much in the world seems to deny your love and frustrate your will.
However difficult it may be though,
help us to trust in your promises,
daring to believe that the day will come,
despite everything that conspires against it,
when your love finally triumphs over all.
Amen.

19

Almighty God,
you tell us to look forward,
anticipating the dawn of your kingdom.
We've no idea when that will be
or what it will mean,
but, however long the wait,
teach us to look forward expectantly,
assured that the day *will* come:
a day that will transform not only our lives,
but the whole world,
for ever.
Amen.

20

Eternal God,
remind us that you alone truly know the future,
your promises of old having found fulfilment in Christ,
the message of the Law and prophets being vindicated by his birth,
death
and resurrection.
Help us,
remembering all you have so faithfully done,
to trust in all you will yet do,
confident that, in the fullness of time,
your purpose will be accomplished
and your kingdom will dawn.
Amen.

21

Almighty God,
we've no problem with praying for the dawn of your kingdom,
for words are easy enough to say,
but when it comes to bringing it closer here on earth
it's a different story,
for suddenly it involves us as well as you –
our willingness to serve,
to love,
to give
and to sacrifice.
We back away,
afraid of what that might demand and cost,
yet you have made clear in Christ that this is what true discipleship means:
not just proclaiming your kingdom but helping to build it,
working in whatever way possible to accomplish your will,
here and now.
Give us a vision not just of the future but also of the present.
Show us what you would have us do
and help us to do it,
so that when we pray 'Your kingdom come',
we may truly mean it.
Amen.

22

Loving God,
we recognise that many were not ready for the coming of Jesus –
many not as prepared as they thought they were,
their lives not what they could have been
and their response not what it should have been.
Help *us* to be prepared –
to live in such a way that at any moment we would be happy to be
confronted by the returning Christ.
Help us to examine ourselves –
our words and deeds,
thoughts and attitudes;
living each day and moment
as though Jesus were visibly by our side
In his name we pray.
Amen.

23

Lord Jesus Christ,
you have given us so much to celebrate,
life to be lived today and every day in all its fullness,
and you warn us against speculating about dates and times we can't predict.
Save us, though, from losing faith in the ultimate fulfilment of your purpose,
in your promise one day to return
and to establish your kingdom on earth as it is in heaven.
May that vision inspire us,
that hope sustain us,
and that assurance shape who we are and how we live.
Amen.

24

Eternal God,
help us to know you now,
love you now,
serve you now –
to live each day as your people,
seeking and honouring your will.
Open our hearts to the reality of your kingdom among us
and teach us more of your way,
so that in everything we do, think and say
we may work to help it grow,
bringing your purpose to fruition.

Learning from all you have done and will yet do,
help us to trust you in the present,
consecrating each moment in faithful discipleship,
to the glory of your name.
Amen.

25
Remind us, Lord,
that you call us not to speculate about the future,
about the date and time of your return,
but simply to trust that eternity is in your hands
and to live each moment in the light of that assurance.
Teach us that the life you offer –
abundant and overflowing –
is not postponed to some distant future
but starts now,
shaped, guided and sustained by your loving hand.
Help us, then, to rejoice and be glad,
living each day wisely and faithfully,
in sure and certain hope.
Amen.

26
Lord Jesus Christ,
prepare our hearts to meet you each and every day,
and when you return in glory to establish your kingdom.
Confront, instruct and enable us by your Spirit,
so that we will be awake and alert,
equipped to live each moment as though the day of your coming has dawned,
and ready to welcome you whenever that might be.
Amen.

27
Teach us, Lord, that you are a God who repeatedly turns the tables;
the way of Christ,
if taken seriously,
challenging the assumptions of this world
and upsetting the status quo.

Teach us that, though it may not sometimes seem like it,
you will finally correct injustice,
overcome evil
and undo wrongs,
in your kingdom the first being last and the last first.
Help us, then, to trust in your purpose,
and to walk humbly with you.
Amen.

28
Lord Jesus Christ,
make us ready, this and every day,
to greet you when you come,
and to live each moment rejoicing in the light of your love.
Amen.

29
As we look forward, Lord, to your coming and coming again,
help us to remember the sacrifice at its heart:
your surrendering yourself for all.
Amen.

30
Living Lord,
whatever life brings,
however demanding it may prove,
and no matter how hard it may sometimes be to understand your will
or to glimpse your hand at work,
help us to keep faith in your purpose,
to trust in your love
and to look forward to the dawn of your kingdom,
living each day in the light of that promise.
Amen.

31
Teach us, Lord, to live each day in the light of your tomorrow;
not simply as though you may one day return
but in the knowledge that, through your Spirit,
you are here already,
and that one day we will meet you face to face.
Amen.

32
Lord Jesus Christ,
we look forward to that day when your kingdom will come
and you are all in all.
Until then, we will trust in you,
secure in your love,
confident in your eternal purpose,
assured that your will shall be done.
To you be praise and glory,
now and for evermore.
Amen.

33
Sovereign God,
thank you that you are not remote from us,
detached in splendid isolation,
but that, having shared our humanity in Christ,
you are with us now,
each moment of every day,
through your Spirit.
Thank you that we can know and see you in the everyday –
through the fellowship of your people,
the world around us
and the circumstances and events of daily life.
Teach us, always, to look beneath the surface,
beyond what we think we know and understand,
and to glimpse your presence in the ordinary and familiar.
Remind us that, through Jesus, heaven has touched earth,
the divine been made human,
the gulf between us overcome.
Amen.

34
Thank you, Lord, for what you have done,
what you are doing
and what you yet shall do.
Thank you that you not only came among us
but are with us now,
constantly at work through your Spirit
to bless, strengthen, guide and call.
Continue to perform in our hearts the miracle of grace,
so that we may know and love you better,
our lives speaking to all of your saving and transforming love.
Amen.

Intercession

35
Gracious God,
we pray for our world,
and those many people who have no thought of Christ or his coming –
those who live only for themselves,
who seek fulfilment solely in material satisfaction,
or who have no spiritual dimension to their lives.
Maranatha!
Come, Lord Jesus, come!

We pray for those who profess to love you
but who have drifted away from your side –
their faith shallow and empty,
their hearts full of bitterness, pride, envy,
or their minds troubled by doubts and disillusionment.
Maranatha!
Come, Lord Jesus, come!

We pray for those who work against your kingdom –
who knowingly cheat and deceive,
who serve self at the cost of others,
who spread hatred and incite violence in pursuit of their aims.
Maranatha!
Come, Lord Jesus, come!

We pray for those who long for your kingdom –
who hunger for a new beginning,
who pray for a fresh chance,
or who simply see no hope for themselves in this world.
Maranatha!
Come, Lord Jesus, come!

And finally we pray for those who work towards your kingdom,
who strive for peace and harmony,
who campaign for freedom and justice,
who demonstrate love and compassion in action.
Maranatha!
Come, Lord Jesus, come!

Gracious God,
we thank you for the assurance that your kingdom will come
and your will be done –
the knowledge that we do not hope or wait in vain.

Teach all your people to live always as those ready for Christ's coming,
so that those who have no faith may hear and respond to your word of
challenge.
Grant to those who despair the knowledge that you are with them,
and to all who work to bring your kingdom nearer
the assurance that in your own time it will come.
In that faith we pray:
Maranatha!
Come, Lord Jesus, come!
Amen.

36
Lord Jesus Christ,
we remember today how so many looked forward to your coming,
but we remember also how it became harder to go on believing as time went
by;
how hope started to splutter and dreams began to die,
until, finally, you came –
the fulfilment of prophecy,
the culmination of God's purpose,
the definitive expression of his love.
Lord of all,
the Word made flesh,
bring hope to your world today.

We remember with gladness how you brought hope throughout your
ministry,
a sense of purpose to those for whom life seemed pointless –
the poor, sick, outcasts and broken-hearted –
light shining in their darkness,
joy breaking into their sorrow,
new beginnings in what had seemed like the end.
Lord of all,
the Word made flesh,
bring hope to your world today.

Hear now our prayer for those caught today in the grip of despair –
those for whom the future seems bleak,
optimism seems foolish,
and trust seems futile.
Reach out in love,
and may light shine into their darkness.
Lord of all,
the Word made flesh,
bring hope to your world today.

Hear our prayer for those whose goals in life have been thwarted,
whose dreams have been shattered,
who have grown weary, cynical and disillusioned.
Reach out in love,
and rekindle their faith in the future.
Lord of all,
the Word made flesh,
bring hope to your world today.

Hear our prayer for those who mourn,
or who wrestle with illness,
or who watch loved ones suffer.
Reach out in love,
and grant them your strength and comfort.
Lord of all,
the Word made flesh,
bring hope to your world today.

Hear our prayer for those whose lives are blighted by injustice,
crushed by oppression, poverty, hunger,
and encourage all who work against the odds to build a better world.
Reach out in love,
and grant the assurance of your coming kingdom.
Lord of all,
the Word made flesh,
bring hope to your world today.

Lord Jesus Christ,
we remember your promise to come again in glory,
the culmination of God's purpose,
the ultimate victory of love.
May that conviction bring new faith,
new vision,
and new purpose wherever life seems hopeless.
Lord of all,
the Word made flesh,
bring hope to your world today.
Amen.

37
Lord Jesus Christ,
at this time supposedly of goodwill among all,
we pray for peace in our world –
an end to division and discord,

hatred and hostility,
death and destruction.
Prince of Peace,
hear our prayer.

Lord Jesus,
we speak of peace
but in our hearts we do not believe it possible.
When we look at our world
we see little hope of an end to its troubles.
We are sceptical,
uncertain,
filled with doubts,
cautious about expressing any optimism.
Even where there are signs of hope,
moves towards reconciliation,
we know it will take many years before we dare believe it is really possible.
But, we pray, in this Advent season,
renew our ability to look forward,
rekindle our belief in the future,
and restore our capacity to hope for better things.
Prince of Peace,
hear our prayer.

Help us –
as we remember your coming,
as we serve you now,
and as we look forward to your coming again –
to anticipate your kingdom through the service we offer
and the lives we live.
Prince of Peace,
hear our prayer.

Teach us to work for that day when your throne will be established,
your justice prevail,
and the earth be filled with the knowledge of you
as the waters cover the sea.
Prince of Peace,
hear our prayer.
Amen.

38

Lord Jesus Christ,
you came to our world,
sharing our humanity,
identifying yourself with us,
expressing through actions and self-sacrifice your love for all.
Lamb of God,
teach us to follow in your footsteps.

Yours was the way of service, compassion and reconciliation.
Despite the rejection of so many,
you saw the best in people,
the good,
the worth that others overlooked.
Lamb of God,
teach us to follow in your footsteps.

You loved all,
without prejudice,
without passing judgement.
Lamb of God,
teach us to follow in your footsteps.

Lord Jesus Christ,
you come to our world still each day,
but to do that fully you need our cooperation,
our willingness to be used for your purpose.
Lamb of God,
teach us to follow in your footsteps.

You need us to speak for you,
to act for you,
to show your love and share your life.
Lamb of God,
teach us to follow in your footsteps.

You need us to take that way of service,
to break down barriers,
to bring people together.
Lamb of God,
teach us to follow in your footsteps.

You need us to take the way of the cross –
valuing people for what they are,
offering them trust and encouragement,
helping them to believe in themselves.
Lamb of God,
teach us to follow in your footsteps.

Lord Jesus Christ,
you came to our world to establish a new kingdom,
a new era,
a new dimension to life.
Help us through who we are
and all we do
to bring that kingdom nearer.
Lamb of God,
teach us to follow in your footsteps.
Amen.

39
The night is turning to day,
darkness is turning to light –
it is time to wake from our sleep.
Wherever there is sorrow, fear, need or hurt,
let us reach out in the name of Christ,
and may his joy and peace,
healing and compassion,
dawn through us, until morning has broken
and the day of his kingdom is here.
Amen.

40
Lord Jesus Christ,
come again into our world
and bring light to those who walk in the night-time of sorrow and despair.
Wherever hearts are broken and spirits crushed,
lives overwhelmed by catastrophe, sickness, war and poverty,
be there in your mercy to bring new beginnings,
the opportunity to start afresh in the hope of a better tomorrow.
Amen.

Reflective prayer

41
I prayed, Lord.
I watched and I waited,
trusting,
expecting,
hoping …
but nothing happened.
I prayed again,
crying out for help,
pleading for guidance,
and this time I was not only sure you'd answer
but also confident of what the answer would be.
Only it wasn't what I expected,
life taking an unforeseen twist,
shattering my illusions,
crushing my hopes,
and leaving faith teetering,
balanced over a precipice.
I called again,
begging you this time,
promising you undying loyalty,
total commitment,
if you would just respond to my plea …
but yet again the answer was wanting,
and I felt lost,
confused,
frightened;
everything that had seemed so certain suddenly so insecure.
But then you spoke –
through the counsel of a friend,
the testimony of Scripture,
the prompting of your Spirit,
the circumstances of life –
and I realised you'd been speaking all along,
giving your reply,
except the answer was different than the one I'd looked for,
your purpose breaking out of the fetters I'd placed upon it,
refusing to be confined.
I'd prayed,
I'd trusted,
but I'd anticipated the wrong thing,
expecting you to act as I wanted
instead of giving myself to your will.

Forgive me, Lord,
and teach me to open my eyes to the unexpected,
to the constant surprise of your love.
Amen.

Closing prayer

42
Gracious God,
just as you came to our world in Christ,
help us now to go out for you,
to proclaim his word,
share his love
and work for his kingdom.
Help us to live in him
and for him
and through him,
until that day when he comes again
and you are all in all.
Amen.

Second week of Advent

43
Gracious God,
reminded at this season of your awesome gift in Christ,
we want to respond,
to offer something in return as a sign of our gratitude
for all you have done and continue to do.
All that we are, Lord,
we bring to you.

We would bring you our worship –
not just well-intentioned thoughts and words
but our wholehearted adoration and joyful thanksgiving.
All that we are, Lord,
we bring to you.

We would bring you our lives –
not just token deeds or outward show,
but hearts consecrated to your service,
embodying your love for all,
your care and compassion for everything you have made.
All that we are, Lord,
we bring to you.

Receive, then, this time set aside for you
as a small yet sincere way of acknowledging your goodness,
and through it equip us to live as your people,
this and every day.
All that we are, Lord,
we bring to you.
Amen.

44
Loving God,
prepare our hearts, for we want to worship you;
prepare our minds, for we want to know you better;
prepare our lives, for we want to serve and honour you.
Hear our prayer,
and move among us.

We come to praise you for your coming to us in Christ,
bringing love,
joy,
peace
and new beginnings.
Hear our prayer,
and move among us.

We come to thank you for your promise that he will come again,
establishing your kingdom and fulfilling your will.
Hear our prayer,
and move among us.

We come seeking pardon for our failure to honour him as we should,
our weak commitment and half-hearted discipleship.
Hear our prayer,
and move among us.

We come to pray for our world of pain and need,
seeking upon it your comfort,
peace,
hope
and renewal.
Hear our prayer,
and move among us.

Meet with us now,
speak your word,
and in the wilderness of our lives make straight a highway for the Lord to
come.
Hear our prayer,
and move among us.
Amen.

45
Lord,
as you spoke through John the Baptist,
and through the prophets before him,
speak afresh through this time of worship.
Speak your word,
and help us to listen.

Behind the voices we hear,
the words we read
and the message we listen to,
may we hear your voice,
calling,
confronting,
leading,
loving,
enthusing
and enabling.
Speak your word,
and help us to listen.

Open our ears, our minds and our souls to your word of truth,
the Word made flesh,
Jesus Christ our Lord.
Speak your word,
and help us to listen.
Amen.

46
Lord Jesus Christ,
prepare your way in our hearts
and make us ready to worship you.
Through our praying, thinking, singing and reading
cleanse our thoughts,
kindle our faith,
renew our commitment
and increase our love,
preparing your way in our lives,
so that we may be ready to follow you faithfully
and serve you more effectively,
to the glory of your name.
Amen.

47
Mighty God,
through the testimony of Scripture,
the experience of fellowship
and the living presence of your Holy Spirit,
give us today a glimpse of your glory,

a deeper insight into who and what you are that stirs our heart
and captures our imagination,
leaving us reeling in wonder
and responding in joyful worship.
Amen.

Praise

48
Lord Jesus Christ,
we praise you today for all those who prepared the way for your coming;
all who made a straight path in the wilderness
so that the hearts of many were ready to receive you.
You call us to prepare your way in turn:
gladly we respond.

We praise you for Abraham who, centuries before your coming,
ventured out in faith,
journeying into the unknown,
trusting in God's promise that all generations would be blessed through his
descendants.
You call us to prepare your way in turn:
gladly we respond.

We praise you for the prophets –
those who foretold your birth,
who looked forward to your kingdom,
and who anticipated your saving grace,
their words bringing hope to countless generations
and still having power to challenge and inspire today.
You call us to prepare your way in turn:
gladly we respond.

We praise you for Mary and Joseph –
for their obedience to your call,
their confidence in your purpose,
their faith that, with you, nothing is impossible.
You call us to prepare your way in turn:
gladly we respond.

We praise you for John the Baptist –
for his willingness to speak the truth
no matter what the cost,
his readiness to point away from himself
and towards your light,
and the integrity of his lifestyle that testified to the truth of his message
in a way that words alone could never begin to.
You call us to prepare your way in turn:
gladly we respond.

We praise you for the Evangelists and apostles –
those who recorded the events of your ministry,
who testified to their experience of your grace;
and who offered guidance in the early days of your Church,
so preparing their own and subsequent generations to respond to your coming
and to look forward in faith to your coming again.
You call us to prepare your way in turn:
gladly we respond.

We praise you for your invitation to continue their ministry –
to witness to your renewing power,
to demonstrate your unfailing compassion,
and to lead others to a knowledge of your redeeming love.
We thank you that, as you have used others,
so now, despite our numerous faults and failings,
you want to use us to promote the growth of your kingdom here on earth.
You call us to prepare your way in turn:
gladly we respond.

Lord Jesus Christ,
help us to make a straight path in the wilderness,
so that the hearts of many may be ready to receive you,
today and every day.
Amen.

49
Father God,
we praise you once more for this season of Advent,
for its mood of expectation,
its message of hope,
its call to prepare ourselves,
its spirit of confidence and trust.
God made flesh,
hear our prayer.

We praise you for the way you have spoken:
in the fulfilment of ancient prophecies,
in promises yet to be realised,
and in the living presence of Christ
made known through his Holy Spirit.
God made flesh,
hear our prayer.

Touch our lives again at this time,
as we remember the coming of Jesus,
as we anticipate his coming again,
and as we strive to serve him better here and now.
God made flesh,
hear our prayer.

Grant that through this season we shall be renewed in hope and
strengthened in faith,
trusting more completely in the future you hold.
May our confidence be deepened in your eternal love and purpose,
despite all that seems to work against it.
And may we be ready to welcome Christ,
in the assurance that as he came so he will come again.
God made flesh,
hear our prayer.
Amen.

Confession

50
Saviour Christ,
we remember today that though your people longed for your coming,
many were not prepared to welcome you,
failing to recognise you when you came.
Lord,
have mercy.

Forgive us that we are equally closed sometimes to your coming into our
lives,
forcing you into a mould we have made for you,
presuming your thoughts and your ways are the same as ours.
Lord,
have mercy.

Forgive us that our expectations are small and limited,
shaped by looking at life from a human rather than eternal perspective.
Lord,
have mercy.

Forgive us, and help us to be prepared:
to examine ourselves –
our words and deeds,
thoughts and attitudes –
and so to live each day open to what you would do in us and through us.
Lord,
have mercy.
Amen.

51
Lord Jesus Christ,
you call us to test ourselves and to ensure that we are still in the faith.
Help us to take that challenge seriously,
for we so easily imagine all is well when in fact much is wrong.
In your mercy,
Lord, forgive us.

We talk of listening to your voice,
but hear what we want to hear.
We speak of seeking your will,
yet we prefer our way,
expecting you to conform to our expectations.
In your mercy,
Lord, forgive us.

Draw close to us and fill us with your Spirit,
so that our faith may be as real and as fresh today as the moment we first
believed.
In your mercy,
Lord, forgive us.

Prepare us for your coming again,
so that we may be ready to receive you
and found faithful in your service.
Amen.

Thanksgiving

52
Sovereign God,
we come before you with awe and wonder,
with reverence, respect and humility,
worshipping you as the beginning and end of all,
the creator of the ends of the earth
and the giver of life and meaning.
For everything you are,
and everything you have done,
Lord, we thank you.

But we come, too, remembering that you took flesh,
entering the world through Christ
and identifying yourself with humankind,
and that you did so not to condemn and punish
but to express the immensity of your love.
For everything you are,
and everything you have done,
Lord, we thank you.

Gratefully, we celebrate your grace,
through which we are able to know, worship and serve you,
assured of your unfailing goodness,
never-ending love
and constant mercy.
For everything you are,
and everything you have done,
Lord, we thank you.
Amen.

Petition

53
Living God,
we remember this day how you prepared the way for your coming:
how to Abraham you promised blessing for all the world through his offspring;
how to your prophets you spoke your word,
promising the Messiah would come,
bringing peace, justice and deliverance for all your people;
how to Elizabeth and Zechariah you promised a son who would prepare the
way of the Lord,
making his way straight in the wilderness;

how to Mary you promised a child who would be called Emmanuel,
God with us,
born to save his people from their sins.
And we remember also how, through John the Baptist,
you announced the fulfilment of those prophecies in the person of Jesus,
the light of the world shining in the darkness.
You promise us that Christ will come again:
prepare our hearts for his coming.

Gracious God,
you spoke your word to so many,
yet when the time came and Jesus was born
so few were ready to receive him.
He was the Word made flesh, but was accused of blasphemy,
he offered life to the world, but was put to death on the cross,
he came to his own people, and they would not receive him.
You promise us that Christ will come again:
prepare our hearts for his coming.

Loving God,
help us as we remember his birth, life, death and resurrection,
to be ready to receive him,
not just when he comes again,
but each day into every part of our lives.
Help us to read your word with new insight,
to offer you our living worship,
and to turn from all that is wrong and faithless in our lives.
Above all help us to focus on what is central to this season
and not on the trappings with which we surround it.
Help us to open our hearts and minds to the guidance of your Holy Spirit,
and respond to his prompting.
Above all, help us to follow in the way of Christ,
loving him as he has loved us.
You promise us that Christ will come again:
prepare our hearts for his coming.
Amen.

54
Redeemer God,
prepare us to worship you:
to recognise your love, mercy, purpose and power,
and to offer our heartfelt praise.
Reach out, Lord,
and make us ready.

Prepare us to serve you:
to understand your will
and to respond to your calling,
consecrating our lives to the growth of your kingdom
in thought,
word
and deed.
Reach out, Lord,
and make us ready.

Prepare us to know you:
to learn more of your goodness, truth and nature,
your work in human history across the years.
Reach out, Lord,
and make us ready.

Prepare us to welcome you:
to live each day,
each moment,
in the light of your promises,
ready to welcome our Saviour Christ when he comes again in glory.
Reach out, Lord,
and make us ready.

Make straight a highway in the wilderness of our lives,
so that he may work in and through us,
by your grace.
Reach out, Lord,
and make us ready.
Amen.

55
Lord Jesus Christ,
be born in us.
Speak to us,
work through us,
shine from us.
Through our service and witness, Lord,
use us for your kingdom.

Take our hands,
our feet,
our lips,
our lives
and use them to your glory.
Through our service and witness, Lord,
use us for your kingdom.

Forgive our faults,
renew our faith,
restore our vision,
receive our service.
Through our service and witness, Lord,
use us for your kingdom.

Come now
and work your miracle of grace within our hearts,
so that we may honour you now
and be ready to welcome you when you come again.
Through our service and witness, Lord,
use us for your kingdom.
Amen.

56
Sovereign God,
we are reminded today of how,
through the prophets and the testimony of John the Baptist,
you brought challenge as well as promise,
a message that disturbed as much as delighted,
unsettled as well as uplifted.
Speak now,
and help us to listen.

Help us,
as we strive to follow Jesus,
to be open to your voice in the wilderness,
your word that probes deep within,
searching the thoughts of the heart
and confronting us with the challenge of the gospel.
Speak now,
and help us to listen.

However demanding it may be,
teach us to hear,
to listen
and to respond.
Speak now,
and help us to listen.
Amen.

57
Gracious God,
help us, like John the Baptist before us
and so many others who have followed in his footsteps,
to see the light of Christ and bear witness to it,
pointing through word and deed to his love for all.
Open our lives, through your Spirit, to his presence among us now,
and help us to live in such a way that his light may shine *in* us
and *through* us,
bringing glory to you.
Amen.

58
Father God,
just as you sent your servant John into the wilderness to prepare the way of
the Lord
and to make ready your people to receive him,
so prepare us now to respond afresh to the gift of Christ
and to all that you offer us through him.
Give us a readiness truly to listen,
to learn,
to worship
and to respond,
receiving the forgiveness he extends
and the renewal he makes possible,
and giving back in return our heartfelt gratitude
expressed in true commitment and faithful service.
Amen.

59
Lord Jesus Christ,
we thank you for all those who prepared the way for your coming,
whether long ago in Bethlehem
or in countless hearts since that day.

Help us to prepare your way in turn,
witnessing to your renewing power
and demonstrating your compassion,
so that the hearts of many may hear your word
and respond to your grace.
Amen.

60
Lord Jesus Christ,
we remember today the ministry of John the Baptist:
his readiness to spend himself in your service,
to proclaim the good news of your kingdom,
to point away from himself
and to seek your glory rather than his own.
Forgive us that we find it so hard to follow his example,
preferring instead the way of self-service,
of putting our own interests before those of others.
Help us to recognise that it is in giving we receive,
and so may we commit our lives to you
and bring glory to your name.
Amen.

61
Are we ready to meet you, Lord?
Prepared for your coming?
If you walked in upon us today,
tomorrow,
the next day,
would our lives measure up to your call,
or would we be embarrassed by your presence,
hastily making excuses to cover our shame at our false and feeble
discipleship?
Remind us that though you do not want us to fret about end times,
you *do* want us to be prepared for your coming,
the promise that you will come again shaping everything we think,
say
and do.
In that knowledge,
may we consecrate every moment to you as though it were our last.
Amen.

62

Awesome God,
save us from carelessness in our relationship with you,
from being casual and complacent in our dealings,
assuming we can gloss over whatever's wrong between us.
Teach us to work at our faith,
preparing the ground each day to know you better,
so that when your kingdom comes we may be ready to stand before you
and meet you,
face to face.
Amen.

63

Lord Jesus Christ,
we know you,
but not as well as we should do;
we have received you into our hearts,
but not as fully as we ought to have done;
we have believed in your name,
but not as completely as you or we would like.
Prepare our hearts now,
and grant us grace upon grace,
so that, glimpsing more of your glory and grasping more of truth,
we will open our hearts again to you,
and welcome you with body, mind and soul
as the Word made flesh,
the Light of the World,
the source and giver of life.
To you be praise and glory,
now and always.
Amen.

64

Help us, Lord, to point to your way,
so that others in turn may find guidance in their journey of life.
May all we say, do, think and are,
point away from us and towards you.
Amen.

65

Lord Jesus Christ,
prepare our hearts to welcome you now,
so that we may be ready to welcome you when you come again.
Amen.

66

Lord Jesus Christ,
teach us to anticipate your return by preparing the way for your coming;
to catch a glimpse of your kingdom through living by its values today.
Live in us now,
so that the day may come when we live with you
and all your people
for all eternity,
your will complete and your promise fulfilled.
Amen.

67

Lord Jesus Christ,
we yearn to serve you,
to honour you,
to love you,
but we are all too conscious that,
just as many were not ready to receive you when first you entered our
world,
so we too can be less prepared than we think,
our narrow expectations
and misplaced assumptions
closing our minds to your presence among us.
So we ask that, as we draw near to you,
you will draw near to us,
stirring our hearts and capturing our imagination.
Prepare us to recognise you afresh at work in our lives and our world,
and so make us ready to serve you,
today and always.
Amen.

68

Lord Jesus Christ,
in all our preparations for Christmas help us to make ready for you
so that we may welcome you more fully into our lives,
both now and on the day of your coming again.
Amen.

69
Living God,
help us in all our preparations for Christmas –
the writing of cards,
buying of presents,
wrapping of gifts,
decorating of the home –
to make ready for you,
preparing ourselves in heart and mind to worship you afresh
and to welcome you more fully into our lives,
so that when the day of your coming finally dawns,
we may be ready to greet you and truly celebrate,
not on *our* terms but on *yours.*
Amen.

Intercession

70
Living God,
thank you for those who have the courage to stand up against evil and
injustice;
those who are ready, if necessary, to stand alone for their convictions,
enduring mockery and rejection,
sacrificing status and security,
willing to risk everything for what they believe to be right.
Thank you for their vision,
their determination,
their willingness to be a voice in the wilderness.
May your glory be revealed,
and all people see it together.

Thank you for those compassionate enough to reach out and help others –
ministering to the sick,
comforting the bereaved,
visiting the lonely,
providing for the poor,
giving hope to the oppressed,
bringing laughter to the sorrowful.
Thank you for their dedication,
their understanding,
their goodness,
their willingness to minister in the wilderness.
May your glory be revealed,
and all people see it together.

You call us to reach out to your broken world –
to those walking in darkness,
wrestling with despair,
craving affection,
thirsting to find purpose in their lives.
Give us faith,
wisdom,
tenderness,
and love to meet that challenge.
Help us to venture into the wilderness ourselves,
and there, gently but confidently,
to speak your word of life.
May your glory be revealed,
and all people see it together.
Amen.

71

Loving God,
we thank you today for the Scriptures,
and the opportunity we have each day to read and study them for ourselves.
Hear now our prayer for all those denied that privilege.

We pray for those who have not heard the challenge of the Bible,
who do not possess a copy of it in their own language,
or who are denied the right to own a Bible or study it freely.
Lord, in your mercy,
hear our prayer.

We pray for those who have heard but closed their minds,
for those who read but do not understand,
and for those who have read the Bible so often it fails to challenge as it used to.
Lord, in your mercy,
hear our prayer.

We pray for those who work to make the Scriptures known and available to all –
those who translate the Bible into modern language and other tongues,
who print and distribute it across the world,
who strive to open its message afresh to each and every generation;
and who preach from it, witnessing to Christ from its pages.
Lord, in your mercy,
hear our prayer.

Loving God,
may your word be made known with clarity, wisdom, faithfulness and
power,
so that many may hear its challenge
and respond in faith to your loving purpose.
Lord, in your mercy,
hear our prayer.
Amen.

Reflective prayer

72
Time to decide?
Come off it, what's the rush?
There's ages yet . . .
no hurry.
I want to live a little first,
let my hair down and enjoy myself.
You're only young once, after all –
time for the serious stuff later.

Time to decide?
Not yet, Lord –
tomorrow will do.
I'm busy right now,
no time to stop –
come back another day.
You understand, don't you?
It's not that I don't want to listen,
but there's the house,
the garden,
the job,
the family –
so much to do
and so little time to do it.
I'll get round to you eventually, I promise.

Time to decide?
But I'm frightened, Lord –
scared of what you might ask,
what committing myself might involve.
I don't like to say no,
but I'm terrified of saying yes,
so give me a little longer,
just a few more days.
Please!

Time to decide?
Do I have to?
I'm happy with the way things are,
quite content to plod along –
why go upsetting the apple cart?
Let's leave it for now, shall we?
Wait until the moment's right?
You don't mind, do you?

Time to decide?
Fair enough, Lord, I'm ready.
What was that?
Too late!
The decision made?
I don't understand what you mean.
Lord, I'm listening.
I'm ready!
Lord?

Closing prayer

73
Lord Jesus Christ,
may we welcome, honour, love and serve you in all we do.
May we know your truth,
do your will
and walk your way;
acknowledging our faults,
receiving your mercy
and responding to your transforming touch.
Equip us to work for you,
witness for you
and *live* for you,
this and every day.
Amen.

Third week of Advent

Approach

74
Lord Jesus Christ,
come among us in this time of worship.
As you came in Bethlehem and will come again in glory,
so, we ask, draw near now
and open our eyes to your presence among us here.
Speak your word,
impart your blessing,
grant your mercy
and renew our faith,
so that we may be ready at every moment to welcome you
and be equipped to live more truly to your praise and glory.
Amen.

Praise

75
Lord Jesus Christ,
we rejoice today that you came in fulfilment of age-old prophecy,
vindicating at last the long-held expectations of your people.
After so many years of frustrated hopes,
so many false dawns and disappointments,
you dwelt among us,
the Prince of Peace,
the promised Messiah,
Son of David,
Son of man,
Son of God.
You have shown us that what God promises shall be accomplished:
we praise you for that assurance.

We rejoice that we are heirs to those promises of old,
for you came not only to your own people
but to the whole human race,
born to set us free from everything that enslaves us
and to open the way to eternal life to anyone willing to follow you.
You have shown us that what God promises shall be accomplished:
we praise you for that assurance.

We rejoice that your purpose for the world continues,
and that the time will come when your kingdom will be established
and your victory be complete.
We thank you that, as you came once, so you will come again;
as you departed into heaven, so you will return in glory,
to establish justice throughout the earth,
and to reconcile all creation through your love.
So we joyfully anticipate that day when there will be no more sorrow or
suffering,
hatred or evil,
darkness or death;
that day when you will be all in all.
You have shown us that what God promises shall be accomplished:
we praise you for that assurance.

Lord Jesus Christ,
we rejoice in this season, so full of promise;
this time which reminds us of all that has been
and all that is yet to be.
May the words we hear today,
the worship we offer
and the events we remember
teach us to trust you completely,
knowing that, whatever else may happen,
your saving purpose will be fulfilled.
You have shown us that what God promises shall be accomplished:
we praise you for that assurance.
Amen.

76
Gracious God,
we praise you today for the power of your word,
the way you have spoken to so many people throughout history.
You called the universe into being –
heaven and earth,
night and day,
the sea and the dry land,
life in its multitude of manifestations.
You spoke,
and it was done,
our world and our very existence being owed to you.
For your word of life,
we praise you.

You called Abraham, Isaac and Jacob,
Moses and Joshua,
judges, kings and prophets,
apostles, disciples, preachers and teachers –
a great company of saints,
each testifying to your sovereign purpose,
your awesome power
and your merciful love;
each hearing your voice and responding in faith.
For your word of life,
we praise you.

You came in Jesus Christ, the Word made flesh,
identifying yourself with our humanity,
sharing our joy and sorrow,
experiencing our life and death.
You came in fulfilment of your promises of old,
revealing the extent of your love
and demonstrating your gracious purpose for all.
For your word of life,
we praise you.

You speak still through the pages of Scripture;
through their record of your involvement in history
and their testimony to your will for the world.
You speak through dialogue between Christians,
through the witness of your Church and personal testimony,
through study and reflection,
and through the sharing of fellowship.
You speak through the grandeur of the universe
and the wonder of life,
your still small voice breaking into our experience to challenge and inspire.
For your word of life,
we praise you.

Gracious God,
we rejoice at the ways you have spoken to us in the past
and the way you continue to speak today.
We receive your word with joyful thanksgiving,
and we pray for strength to make it so much a part of us
that your voice may be heard through all we are and do.
For your word of life,
we praise you.
Amen.

77
Loving God,
from earliest times you have been at work in our world,
striving to fulfil your purposes,
preparing the way for the coming of your kingdom.
With glad thanksgiving,
we worship you.

We praise you for the witness of the prophets
foretelling the coming of the Messiah.
With glad thanksgiving,
we worship you.

We praise you for the ministry of John the Baptist,
a voice in the wilderness calling people to repentance,
making ready the way of the Lord.
With glad thanksgiving,
we worship you.

We praise you for those who made the gospel known to us,
giving us the opportunity to respond.
With glad thanksgiving,
we worship you.

Help us now truly to prepare for Christmas,
not simply outwardly but inwardly,
so that we may joyfully celebrate the birth of Christ
and receive him into our lives.
With glad thanksgiving,
we worship you.
Amen.

78
Loving God,
we celebrate today the fulfilment of your word across the years.
You promised Abraham that through his offspring
all the earth would be blessed –
and it was.
With joyful hearts,
we praise you.

You promised through your prophets that the Messiah would come . . .
and he came.
With joyful hearts,
we praise you.

You promised Mary that she would give birth to a son . . .
and she did.
With joyful hearts,
we praise you.

You promised the disciples that death would not be the end . . .
and it wasn't.
With joyful hearts,
we praise you.

You promised your followers that they would receive the Holy Spirit . . .
and it happened.
With joyful hearts,
we praise you.

Teach us, then, to trust you for the present and the future,
knowing that you are always faithful,
and that you will accomplish whatever you have pledged to do.
Teach us to be faithful to you in all our dealings,
just as you are invariably faithful to us.
With joyful hearts,
we praise you.
Amen.

79
Gracious God,
we praise you for this season of Advent –
this time for rejoicing and celebration,
adoration and thanksgiving –
and we exult in your goodness.
Receive our homage.
Receive our worship.

We praise you for coming in Christ,
bringing in a new kingdom
and anticipating an era of peace and justice
when the poor will have plenty,
the hungry be fed,
and the lowly be lifted up.
Receive our homage.
Receive our worship.

We praise you that you want us to be a part of that,
not just to share in it but also to play a part in bringing it to pass.
Receive our homage.
Receive our worship.

Forgive us that we sometimes lose sight of your purpose
and underestimate your greatness.
Open our eyes to the breadth of your love,
the wonder of your mercy
and the extent of your goodness,
and so may we give you the worship and adoration that is due to you,
this and every day.
Receive our homage.
Receive our worship.
Amen.

Confession

80
Sovereign God,
we thank you for your word –
recorded in Scripture
and handed down over countless generations;
heard through reading, preaching, fellowship and worship;
glimpsed in the beauty of our world and the mysteries of life;
brought to life through prayer and meditation,
embodied through Jesus Christ, the Word made flesh.
Speak again now,
and give us ears to hear.

Forgive us that we are sometimes slow to listen.
We do not make time to read the Scriptures as we should,
allowing instead the pressures and responsibilities of life,
our many interests, pleasures and concerns,
to crowd out the time we spend with you.
Speak again now,
and give us ears to hear.

We become casual or complacent in our worship,
no longer expecting you to challenge us,
no longer moved to a sense of awe,
no longer hungry for spiritual food.
Speak again now,
and give us ears to hear.

We neglect the opportunity for fellowship,
turning in on ourselves,
imagining we know all there is to know of you,
more concerned with our own insights than with those we can gain from others.
Speak again now,
and give us ears to hear.

We grow deaf to your voice in creation,
our senses dulled by over-familiarity,
and have no time to pause and ponder,
to reflect on deeper, eternal realities.
Speak again now,
and give us ears to hear.

We believe we have listened and responded,
but our focus is on the written word rather than the Word made flesh,
the letter rather than the spirit of your revelation in Christ.
Speak again now,
and give us ears to hear.

Sovereign God,
speak afresh through the pages of Scripture,
through the worship we share,
through the experience and insight of other Christians,
and, above all, through the inner presence of the living Christ in our hearts.
Teach us, when your voice seems silent,
to listen again more carefully,
and to rediscover your word.
Speak again now,
and give us ears to hear.
Amen.

81
Loving God,
we thank you for the great truth at the heart of this season –
your coming to our world in Christ.
Open our hearts now,
and help us truly to welcome you.

We praise you that you go on coming,
day after day,
not just to others but also to us,
meeting and working within us through your Holy Spirit.
Open our hearts now,
and help us truly to welcome you.

Forgive us everything that obstructs your coming –
all the trivia and irrelevancies with which we fill our lives
at the cost of time for you;
all the cares, doubts and unbelief
that prevent us sometimes from even glimpsing your presence.
Open our hearts now,
and help us truly to welcome you.

Come afresh into our lives,
and break through all the barriers we erect against you,
so that we may know you more nearly by our side
and draw closer to you than we have ever been before.
Open our hearts now,
and help us truly to welcome you.

Speak your word,
grant your guidance,
confer your power
and fill us with your love,
so that we may serve you as faithfully
as you have served us in Christ.
Open our hearts now,
and help us truly to welcome you.
Amen.

Thanksgiving

82
Thank you, Lord, that in a world where promises are two a penny,
made today and broken tomorrow,
where so little can be relied on to deliver what it purports to offer,
we can put our trust in your promises
and be confident they will be honoured.
Faithful God,
thank you.

Through the prophets you foretold the coming of the Messiah,
a Saviour and Redeemer,
and in Christ you fulfilled that pledge,
your Word being made flesh among us.
Faithful God,
thank you.

He told his followers that though he would die he would rise again,
and they met him,
just as he had said:
risen,
alive,
victorious.
Faithful God,
thank you.

You promise us in turn your guidance,
strength,
mercy
and peace;
above all, life now and for evermore.
Faithful God,
thank you.

Teach us to put our trust in you,
confident that though all else may fail,
you will not.
Faithful God,
thank you.
Amen.

83
Sovereign God,
we thank you that you are a God on whom we can depend;
a God in whom we can put our trust.
What you promise, you do;
what you purpose, you accomplish.

We remember your promise to Abraham:
that, through his offspring, all the world would be blessed;
to Moses:
that you would lead the Israelites out of Egypt;
to Isaiah:
that you would deliver your people from exile;
to your prophets:
that the Messiah would come;
to the apostles:
that he would rise again on the third day.
What you promise, you do;
what you purpose, you accomplish.

We thank you that you fulfilled those promises, just as you said you would –
your Son arising from the line of Abraham;
your chosen nation set free from slavery;
your people returning joyfully to Jerusalem,
your promised deliverer born in Bethlehem;
your power seen in the resurrection of Christ.
What you promise, you do;
what you purpose, you accomplish.

We thank you for what that means for us today –
that we can live each moment with confidence,
whatever our circumstances may be,
whatever times of testing may befall us,
knowing that, though all else may fail, you will not;
though heaven and earth may pass away,
your words will endure for ever.
What you promise, you do;
what you purpose, you accomplish.

So we look forward to that day when your purpose is fulfilled
and you are all in all,
and, until then, we will trust in you,
secure in your love,
confident in your eternal purpose,
assured that your will shall be done.
What you promise, you do;
what you purpose, you accomplish.
Thanks be to God.
Amen.

84
Saviour Christ,
thank you for promises of old foretelling your coming,
for the testimony of the Gospels to your birth in Bethlehem,
for the witness of Scripture to your life-changing power,
for the experience of those across the ages called to be your Church.
But, above all, thank you that we can know you for ourselves,
believing not just *about* you but *in* you as we joyfully respond to your love.
You have called us to an adventure of faith.
Help us to explore it with you.
Amen.

Petition

85

Loving God,
we remember today how prophets foretold the coming of Christ –
how they declared their faith in your purpose,
their confidence in your love,
their assurance of your final victory.
They did not keep their faith to themselves;
they shared it with others:
teach us to do the same.

We remember how shepherds responded to the message of the angels –
how they hurried to Bethlehem
and found the baby lying in a manger,
and how they went on their way praising and glorifying you
for everything they had seen and heard.
They did not keep their faith to themselves;
they shared it with others:
teach us to do the same.

We remember how John the Baptist prepared the way of Christ in the
wilderness –
how he proclaimed a baptism of repentance,
a new beginning,
the coming of one far greater than he could ever be.
He did not keep his faith to himself;
he shared it with others:
teach us to do the same.

We remember how you came to us in Christ –
how he brought light into our darkness,
hope into our despair,
joy into our sorrow.
He did not live his life *for* himself.
He did not keep his faith *to* himself;
he shared it with others:
teach us to do the same.
Amen.

86
Lord Jesus Christ,
promised of old,
foretold by prophets,
long awaited by your people,
prepare a way in our hearts so that you may more fully enter in.
Come now,
and be born in our hearts afresh.

Saviour Christ,
rejected and despised,
nailed to a cross and sealed in a tomb,
break down the barriers of doubt and disbelief that keep us from you –
the faults and failings that deny your love and obstruct your purpose.
Come now,
and be born in our hearts afresh.

Risen Christ,
here through your Spirit,
here by our side,
fill us with your love,
redeem us by your grace
and renew us by your power.
Come now,
and be born in our hearts afresh.

Sovereign Christ,
coming to redeem your people,
to reign in glory and to welcome us into your kingdom,
make your path straight within us,
so that, consecrated to your service,
we in turn may help to prepare your way in the lives of others.
Come now,
and be born in our hearts afresh.
Amen.

87
Living God,
we recall today how you have guided your people across the years,
leading them from earliest times.
Show us your way,
and help us to follow in turn.

We recall how you called Abraham to venture out into the unknown,
Moses to lead your people out of Egypt,
and Joshua to take them into the Promised Land;
how you called kings to rule over them
and judges and prophets to speak your word.
Show us your way,
and help us to follow in turn.

We recall how you called shepherds in the fields
and wise men from the East
to go to Bethlehem to see the Christ-child,
how, in Christ, you chose twelve ordinary people to be disciples
and how, on the Damascus Road, you called Paul to become Apostle to the Gentiles.
Show us your way,
and help us to follow in turn.

We recognise how you have spoken to countless others across the years,
often calling less directly,
but guiding just as surely,
confronting through your word,
inspiring through your love,
enabling through your power,
renewing through your grace.
Show us your way,
and help us to follow in turn.

Open our eyes in turn to all the ways you continue to prompt;
open our ears to the ways you speak,
open our lives to the way you guide,
and help us to respond.
Show us your way,
and help us to follow in turn.
Amen.

88
Eternal God,
we *say* we believe in your promises,
but sometimes we are not as sure as we'd like to be.
Lord, we believe,
help with our unbelief.

When it comes to stepping out in faith,
taking risks for your kingdom;
to receiving mercy,
and accepting we are truly forgiven;
to death and resurrection,
holding firm to the assurance you have given of life beyond the grave,
we *do* believe,
but our trust is fragile,
threatened by doubts and questions,
at risk of being broken.
Lord, we believe,
help with our unbelief.

Remind us of all you have already done across the years,
the promises you have so wonderfully honoured
and prophecies so gloriously fulfilled.
Remind us of the words we personally have found to be true
and of the faithfulness that so many have experienced first-hand in turn.
Lord, we believe,
help with our unbelief.

So may we put our hands in yours
and hold on to you more firmly,
assured deep in our hearts that your word is true,
your love constant
and your promises sure.
Lord, we believe,
help with our unbelief.
Amen.

89
Living God,
speak again in this Advent season of your redeeming love,
your desire to forgive,
restore
and renew.
Speak your word,
and help us to listen.

Speak of the unfolding of your purpose through law and prophets,
gloriously fulfilled in the birth of your Son
and in his living, dying and resurrection.
Speak your word,
and help us to listen.

Speak of his coming again to establish your kingdom,
to rule on earth and in heaven,
and to raise us to newness of life lived for ever with you.
Speak your word,
and help us to listen.

Prepare our hearts to listen,
to learn,
to reflect,
to respond,
and so may this time draw us closer to you,
by your grace deepening our faith
and strengthening our commitment.
Speak your word,
and help us to listen.
Amen.

90
Living God,
you spoke,
and the world was brought into being –
the heavens and the earth,
the sea and dry land,
night and day,
life in all its variety and abundance.
Speak again,
and help us to hear you.

You spoke again in the book of the Law,
the poetry of the psalms,
the wisdom of the teacher,
the chronicling of history
and the message of the prophets,
revealing your will,
proclaiming your purpose.
Speak again,
and help us to hear you.

You spoke through Jesus Christ, the Word made flesh,
through those who witnessed to his life and ministry,
and through those who across the years have shared in the building of his
Church.
Speak again,
and help us to hear you.

You have spoken throughout history:
through preaching and teaching,
through study and quiet devotion,
through prayer and fellowship,
through the wonder of this world;
and still you speak today,
your word ever old but always new,
able to redeem, renew and restore.
Speak again,
and help us to hear you.

Speak to us now, we pray.
Help us to use this season of Advent to listen more carefully to your voice,
and so to walk with you more closely,
this and every day.
Speak again,
and help us to hear you.
Amen.

91
Gracious God,
we come to reflect again on your age-old promises,
on your sovereign purpose,
on your constant working within human history.
As we worship,
deepen our faith.

We remember that you brought this world into being,
that you guided your people across the centuries,
despite repeated rebellion and disobedience,
and that, through your great love,
you took on human flesh,
coming to our world through Jesus Christ.
As we worship,
deepen our faith.

We rejoice in all he showed of you
through his birth in Bethlehem,
his life and ministry,
his death and resurrection,
and we celebrate his living presence with us now through his Spirit.
As we worship,
deepen our faith.

Open our hearts to everything you would say to us through this day,
so that we may understand your love more completely
and serve you more faithfully.
Amen.

92

Remind us, Lord, that you alone truly know the future,
your promises of old having found fulfilment in Christ,
the message of the law and prophets vindicated by his birth, death and
resurrection.
Help us, remembering all you have so faithfully done,
to trust in all you will yet do,
confident that, in the fullness of time,
your will shall be done and your kingdom come.
Amen.

93

When we look at the world, Lord –
its tensions and suffering, need and heartbreak –
it's hard not to wonder what you're doing
and why you take so long to put things right,
for much there seems to question your love
and undermine your will.
Help us to understand, though,
that there are no quick fixes to such things,
no short-term solutions,
but that you are working nonetheless,
your purpose destined to triumph,
not in *our* time,
but in *yours*.
Amen.

94

Faithful God,
teach us to step out in faith,
trusting in your word,
seeking your will
and offering our commitment,
so that we may recognise more fully the nearness of your presence,
the truth of your promises,
the constancy of your love
and the wonder of your grace.
Amen.

95
Eternal God,
ruler of history,
Lord of space and time,
teach us to wait upon you, now and always,
trusting that, though we may not always see it,
you are constantly at work,
bringing your saving purpose to fulfilment in Christ.
Amen.

96
Loving God,
teach us that your gracious purpose goes back to the beginning of time,
and that it will endure until the end of time,
and beyond.
Amen.

97
Gracious God,
you tell us that your word was active from the beginning
and will continue until the end of time;
that it brought life itself into existence,
and controls the destiny of everything you have created;
that what you have decreed, will be,
for no word of yours returns to you empty.
Help us, then, to listen to what you would say to us
both today and throughout this season of Advent.
Open our ears, our hearts and our minds,
so that we may hear your voice and respond in joyful service.
Amen.

98
Eternal God,
we celebrate today the fulfilment of your promises of old
through the coming of the Messiah,
foretold by the prophets and long yearned for –
a Saviour to deliver your people and establish your kingdom,
bringing freedom, life and new beginnings.
We celebrate how wonderfully you honoured those promises in Christ,
granting through him more than we can ever ask or imagine.

Help us now, as we worship you, to celebrate your faithfulness
and to trust you completely for the future,
knowing that we can depend on you, come what may,
certain that what you have pledged will be accomplished
and that nothing can ever separate us from your love in Jesus Christ our Lord.
Amen.

99
Sovereign God
we thank you for all who have borne witness to your coming in Christ,
all who have shared their faith
so that others might come to know him and experience his love for
themselves.
We thank you for those from whom we first heard the gospel,
and all who have nurtured and encouraged us in discipleship.
Help us now to play our part in that continuing ministry,
sharing what Christ means to us with those around us,
and making known the way he has worked in our lives.
Send us out in his name, to his glory.
Amen.

100
Loving God,
we praise you for fulfilling your age-long purpose through the birth of Jesus.
We thank you that your promises are not simply empty words,
like so many of ours,
but pledges we can rely on,
knowing they will always be honoured.
Teach us, then, to read the Scriptures
hearing your word revealed in Christ
and trusting in the promise of new life you have given us through him.
Amen.

101
Gracious God,
we thank you for the gift of words
through which we are able to express so much.
We thank you for the words of Scripture that speak so powerfully of your love.
But most of all we thank you for putting your words into action,
making them come alive in the person of Jesus.

Help us in our turn not simply to use words
but to act upon them,
not just to talk about faith
but to live it day by day.
Amen.

Intercession

102
Loving God,
accept our glad thanksgiving for all you have given us,
and hear now our prayers for your world.
We pray for those for whom there is no celebration –
the poor and the hungry,
the homeless and the sick,
the lonely and the bereaved,
the oppressed and the persecuted.
Lord, you call us to respond to their need:
help us to reach out in love.

We pray for all those whose celebration is marred by fear –
those who are anxious for themselves or a loved one,
who see no hope in the future,
or who live under the constant threat of danger.
Lord, you call us to respond to their need:
help us to reach out in love.

We pray for all who wrestle with grief –
those whose lives have been broken by tragedy,
who live each day in perpetual shadow,
crushed by the burden of sorrow.
Lord, you call us to respond to their need:
help us to reach out in love.

We pray for all who feel isolated –
those who feel unloved, unwanted,
who find it hard to show love towards others,
or whose relationships have been broken by cruelty, discord, division.
Lord, you call us to respond to their need:
help us to reach out in love.

Loving God,
may your light reach into the darkest places of the world,
so that there may be hope rather than despair,
joy rather than sorrow,
and love rather than hatred.
Come now to our world through Jesus Christ,
to bring good news to the poor,
release to the captives,
recovery of sight to the blind,
and to let the oppressed go free.
Lord, you call us to respond to their need:
help us to reach out in love.
Amen.

103
Awesome and astonishing God,
may a vision of your greatness burn brightly in our hearts,
inspiring faith, joy, trust and peace,
and showing itself in love for you and service to all,
through Jesus Christ our Lord.
Amen.

104
Lord Jesus Christ,
light of the world,
break into the darkness that oppresses so many.
Bring love where there is hatred,
good where there is evil,
and hope where there is despair,
your grace creating peace instead of war,
freedom instead of oppression,
joy instead of sorrow
and life instead of death.
Come now,
and shine in the hearts of all.
Amen.

Reflective prayer

105
Living God,
I thought I'd responded,
that I'd professed my faith and offered my commitment,
but I hadn't,
not fully,
not as you wanted me to.
I'd offered a part of me,
but the rest was still firmly mine,
ring-fenced,
not to be disturbed,
kept quietly away from any challenge you might bring.
I was ready to serve,
so long as your goals were mine;
ready to follow,
so long as our paths coincided,
but the thought of loving proving costly,
discipleship bringing demands,
well, quite simply I pushed it aside,
hoping that what I couldn't see I could safely ignore.
Only I couldn't,
for instead of having a foot in both camps,
I didn't have one in either,
life lived neither fully for me nor for you.
Forgive me, Lord,
and teach me to consecrate myself wholly to your service:
to be used as you would use me,
to serve as you would have me serve,
confident that though I may not have the resources needed,
your strength will see me through.
Amen.

Closing prayer

106
Go now in joy and peace,
and the blessing of Jesus Christ –
Light of the world and Light of life –
be with you this day and for all eternity.
Amen.

Fourth week of Advent

Approach

107
Lord Jesus Christ,
born to Mary,
coming to our world through her,
be born afresh in us
that we might be born again through you.
Lord, hear us,
graciously hear us.

Touch now this time of worship
that the message of your birth,
so familiar and well loved,
will speak afresh with new power and clarity,
thrilling our hearts
and filling us with joy and gratitude.
Lord, hear us,
graciously hear us.

Draw close to us now,
that through welcoming you into our lives
and opening ourselves once more to your renewing power
you may reach out through us to the world,
bringing hope and healing, light and life,
to the glory of your name.
Lord, hear us,
graciously hear us.
Amen.

108
Almighty God,
we recall at this joyful season how,
through her willingness to hear your word
and commit herself to your service,
you were able to use Mary to fulfil your purpose,
entering our world,

inaugurating your kingdom
and bringing closer that day when sorrow and suffering,
darkness and death will be no more.
Take what we are,
and direct what we shall be.

Help us, then, as we gather now to worship,
to hear your word
and to respond with similar obedience,
prepared to be used as you see fit.
Take what we are,
and direct what we shall be.

Through our discipleship,
weak and feeble though it might be,
may your grace be revealed,
your love made known
and your world enriched.
Take what we are,
and direct what we shall be.
Amen.

109
Loving God,
though much in this season is familiar and traditional,
help us to meet you through it,
hearing your word for our lives,
grasping your purpose more fully
and glimpsing the awesome extent of your love,
so that the one born in Bethlehem so long ago
may be born in our hearts today.
Touch this service by your grace,
that all we share in may gladden our hearts,
thrill our souls
and enlighten our lives,
leading us to an experience of your living presence
and saving power,
through Jesus Christ our Lord.
Amen.

110
Living God,
open your word to us,
that it may be a lamp to our feet,
and open our hearts to you,
that you may lighten our path.
Shine upon us through your Spirit,
that we shall be awake at every moment to your guidance
and conscious of your presence daily by our side,
through Jesus Christ our Lord.
Amen.

Praise

111
Lord Jesus Christ,
fulfilment of age-old promises,
of the words of the prophets,
of your people's ancient hope,
we worship you.
Great is your name,
and greatly to be praised.

Infant Christ,
laid in a manger,
born in a stable,
outcast and stranger from the very beginning,
yet inextinguishable light of the world,
we adore you.
Great is your name,
and greatly to be praised.

Suffering Christ,
bruised and broken,
cut down from a cross and laid in a tomb,
we acclaim you.
Great is your name,
and greatly to be praised.

Victorious Christ,
with us through your Spirit,
walking among us,
we welcome you.
Great is your name,
and greatly to be praised.

Exalted Christ,
enthroned in splendour,
ruling on high,
and waiting to welcome us into your kingdom,
we thank you.
Great is your name,
and greatly to be praised.

Make us ready,
this and every day,
to greet you when you come,
and to live each moment rejoicing in the light of your love.
Great is your name,
and greatly to be praised.
Amen.

112
Living God,
for revealing yourself in Christ,
we praise you.
In his name,
receive our worship.

For coming among us through him,
walking our earth,
identifying yourself with what it means to be human,
we thank you.
In his name,
receive our worship.

For his life and ministry,
words and deeds,
death and resurrection,
and the knowledge that, through his Spirit, he is with us still,
we adore you.
In his name,
receive our worship.

Open our hearts again to his searching challenge,
healing touch
and transforming power,
and, by his grace,
help us to know him better.
In his name,
receive our worship.
Amen.

113
Almighty God,
you are greater than our minds can fathom,
higher than our highest thoughts,
sovereign over all,
worthy of praise and honour.
Great is your name.
Gladly we worship you!

Forgive us that we sometimes lose our sense of awe and wonder in your presence,
oblivious to your greatness and forgetful of your goodness.
Great is your name.
Gladly we worship you!

Speak to us,
as you spoke to Mary,
and help us to catch a new sense of who you are,
of what you have done,
and of all you will yet do in our lives.
Great is your name.
Gladly we worship you!

Help us to magnify your name,
singing your praises,
telling of your greatness
and living to your glory.
Great is your name.
Gladly we worship you!
Amen.

114
Loving God,
help us to consecrate every moment to you,
everything we do and say,
every aspect of our lives.
Help us to know and love you better,
so that we may be ready to hear you,
ready to serve you,
and ready to celebrate that day when your will is done
and your kingdom comes in all its glory.
Amen.

Confession

115

Loving God,
the great festival of Christmas is drawing nearer
and we are busy preparing for it –
choosing presents,
writing cards,
planning get-togethers,
buying food –
so much that has become an accepted and expected part of this season.
Yet, in all the bustle, we so easily forget the most important thing of all:
responding to the wonderful gift of your Son.
You have come to us in Christ:
forgive us when we fail to receive him.

We tell ourselves that *we* are different –
that we will be worshipping you day by day,
sharing in services of lessons and carols,
hearing again familiar and well-loved verses of Scripture,
but we know that this isn't enough in itself,
for these too can become just another part of our traditional celebrations,
washing over us rather than communicating the great message of the gospel.
We become so concerned with the wrapping
that we fail to recognise the gift concealed underneath.
You have come to us in Christ:
forgive us when we fail to receive him.

Forgive us for relegating Jesus to the periphery of our celebrations,
rather than placing him at the centre where he belongs;
for turning this season into a time for material extravagance,
rather than an opportunity for spiritual fulfilment;
for doing so much to prepare for Christmas on the surface,
yet so little to make ourselves ready within.
You have come to us in Christ:
forgive us when we fail to receive him.

Loving God,
open our hearts now to hear again your word,
to welcome the living Christ,
and to reflect on our response to his call.
May this Advent season teach us to welcome him afresh into our lives
and to rejoice in his love not just at Christmas
but always.
You have come to us in Christ:
forgive us when we fail to receive him.
Amen.

116
Forgive us, Lord,
for so often we're disobedient,
ignoring your call and defying your will,
preferring our way to yours.
Teach us, instead, like Mary long ago,
to listen to your voice and humbly to obey,
putting your will before our own –
self second and you first.
Amen.

117
Lord Jesus Christ,
for our failure to welcome you as we should,
our keeping you at arm's length,
our resistance to your will,
forgive us.
Overcome our disobedience,
our apathy and weakness,
and help us to give you the place you deserve,
at the centre of our lives.
Amen.

Thanksgiving

118
Gracious God,
we thank you for this glad season:
for its news of great joy for all people;
its message of hope, peace, love and new beginnings.
Gratefully,
we worship you.

We thank you for the humility of Mary,
the faith of Joseph,
the proclamation of the angels
and the joy of the shepherds –
the way you changed their lives for ever.
Gratefully,
we worship you.

Above all, though,
we thank you that you have changed *our* lives too;
that the good news these heard and responded to long ago
is news still today –
as special now as then,
and for *us* as much as anyone!
Gratefully,
we worship you.

Teach us never to forget that wonderful truth;
never to overlook the fact that you have come to us in Christ.
May that knowledge burn brightly in our hearts,
a constant source of joy and inspiration,
whatever life may bring.
Gratefully,
we worship you.
Amen.

119

Thank you, Lord, for the closeness you make possible with you,
the relationship you have opened up through your coming among us,
sharing our humanity
and dying our death to bring us life.
Help us to celebrate the love at the heart of this season –
your gift of Christ –
and, through him,
draw us closer to you each day.
Amen.

120

Loving God,
though much of the packaging surrounding Christmas needs discarding,
save us from overlooking the love you showed in preparing the way of
Christ.
Help us,
if we would fully celebrate your gift,
to appreciate the context in which you gave it –
the history of your people,
the teaching of the Law,
and the message of the prophets,
each finding glorious fulfilment in the Word made flesh.
For your Son,
and all that points to him and your love,
thank you!
Amen.

Petition

121

Living God,
you promised to come to your people of old through the advent of the
Messiah.
You promise to come to each of us in the triumphant and glorious return of
your Son.
So then, we ask:
open our hearts to your coming in Christ.

Loving God,
you came into our world through Mary,
entering our world of space and time.
You want to come afresh through each of us,
Jesus made real in our day-to-day lives.
So then, we ask:
open our hearts to your coming in Christ.

Gracious God,
you needed Mary's assent before you could work through her.
You need our willingness to let you work through us.
So then, we ask:
open our hearts to your coming in Christ.

Sovereign God,
you called Mary to believe that with you nothing is impossible.
You need us to show that same faith if your kingdom is to come.
So then, we ask:
open our hearts to your coming in Christ.

Mighty God,
you brought a new beginning to Mary,
to Joseph,
to your people Israel,
to all the world.
You offer a new beginning to each of us,
this and every day.
So then, we ask:
open our hearts to your coming in Christ.
Amen.

122

Eternal God,
you came to our world not in a blaze of publicity,
surrounded by pomp and show,
nor to the frenzied acclaim of crowds gathered to greet your coming,
but quietly,
unassumingly,
almost unnoticed,
in the quiet of the night in the little town of Bethlehem –
born in a manger,
to the Virgin Mary,
your coming first witnessed by shepherds out working in the fields.
As the heavens are higher than the earth,
so our ways are not your ways,
nor our thoughts your thoughts.

Time and again you have chosen the small,
the humble,
the insignificant,
and worked out your purposes through them.
You have shown your strength in what the world counts weakness,
you have made the last first, and the least the greatest.
As the heavens are higher than the earth,
so our ways are not your ways,
nor our thoughts your thoughts.

Teach us what that means today –
that you can use us beyond our imagining,
that you can take what seems unimportant
and turn it into something wonderful,
that you can work among us in ways that exceed our wildest expectations.
Teach us to see life not merely from our own perspective
but from yours,
and so may your strength be made perfect in our weakness.
As the heavens are higher than the earth,
so our ways are not your ways,
nor our thoughts your thoughts.
Amen.

123

Loving God,
we grow tired of most things eventually,
even those that are special.
Meet us afresh,
and rekindle our faith.

What once captured our imagination,
sending a tingle down our spine,
now leaves us cold;
what formerly filled us with delight
now passes us by.
Meet us afresh,
and rekindle our faith.

Save us from growing over-familiar with the message of your love,
from losing our sense of wonder and gratitude at everything you have done
in Christ.
May the good news of his birth,
the glad tidings of his life and ministry,
and the gospel of his death and resurrection
speak afresh to us each day,
moving us to joyful praise and heartfelt worship.
Meet us afresh,
and rekindle our faith.
Amen.

124
Gracious God,
you came to our world in fulfilment of your promises of old,
your word embodied in a child lying in a manger.
Come again now,
and be born in our hearts.

You loved us so much that,
to break down the barriers that keep us from you,
you staked everything,
surrendering your all.
Come again now,
and be born in our hearts.

You shared our humanity from birth to death,
so that with you we might share your eternity,
life in all its fullness.
Come again now,
and be born in our hearts.

You became God with us,
so that we might become one with *you.*
Come again now,
and be born in our hearts.

Teach us that, as you needed Mary's response then,
you long for *our* response now:
our willingness to accept your mercy
and to experience the blessings you so long to give us.
Come again now,
and be born in our hearts.

Fill us with your presence deep within,
so that we may truly love you and joyfully serve you,
this and every day.
Come again now,
and be born in our hearts.
Amen.

125
Father God,
thank you for becoming one with us so that we might become one with you;
for entering our world so that we might enter your kingdom,
for dying our death so that we might live your life.
You have drawn close in Christ.
Draw us closer now to you.

Thank you for the knowledge that you took on our flesh and walked
our earth,
identifying yourself fully with humankind,
sharing our flesh and blood.
You have drawn close in Christ.
Draw us closer now to you.

Above all,
thank you for the assurance that you are with us now,
here through your Spirit;
and for the promise that you will be with us always,
nothing finally able to separate us from your love.
You have drawn close in Christ.
Draw us closer now to you.

Help us to recognise your presence with us each moment,
always seeking to know you better,
until that day when we know you fully
even as we are fully known.
You have drawn close in Christ.
Draw us closer now to you.
Amen.

126

Redeemer God,
as we prepare to celebrate the birth of your Son,
speak through the singing of hymns,
the reading of Scripture,
the preaching of your word,
the offering of prayers –
these and so much more.
Speak your word,
and help us to listen.

Break through all that separates us from you and him:
over-familiarity,
indifference,
self-will,
disobedience,
narrowness of vision,
weakness of resolve.
Speak your word,
and help us to listen.

Move among us through your Spirit –
inspiring,
instructing,
revealing,
renewing –
so that we may be equipped to worship and serve you.
Speak your word,
and help us to listen.
Amen.

127

Gracious God,
you may not ask of us what you asked of Mary,
but your challenge comes nonetheless
calling us to avenues of service we would never imagine possible.
Whoever we are,
we all have a part to play in your purpose.
Grant us the humility we need to hear your voice
and the faith we need to respond.
Like Mary,
let each of us be ready to answer when you call:
'I am the Lord's servant.
Let it be to me just as you say.'
Amen.

128

Lord Jesus Christ,
open our hearts, minds and souls to your presence,
so that we may know you better
and follow you more faithfully.
Through the reading of Scripture,
the prompting of your Spirit,
the sharing of fellowship
and the experiences of daily life,
offer a lamp for our path,
and a torch to our way.
Guide us in our journey of discipleship,
so that in you,
the Lord of life and Light of the world,
we may find *our* Lord and *our* Light,
with us this day and always.
Amen.

129

Almighty God,
teach us to see your glory in your holiness,
your creative power,
your purity, righteousness, justice and truth –
a God set apart,
higher than our highest thoughts,
greater than we can fully understand –
but teach us also to see it in the radiance of Christ,
the light of his love, mercy, grace and compassion,
reaching out to heal and bless, forgive and restore –
a God sharing our humanity,
walking our earth,
closer than our closest friend
and more wonderful that we can ever imagine:
the servant yet Lord of all.
Help us to live each day in the light of your awesome power
that fills our universe,
yet touches our lives,
that is before and beyond all,
yet has infinite time and love for each one of us –
a glory like no other.
Amen.

130

Gracious God,
teach us to seek not our glory but yours,
not our will but your purpose,
not our well-being but your kingdom.
Use us as you see fit,
in your service.
Amen.

131

Loving God,
for all our faith
there are some things we consider beyond us,
and beyond you.
Belief says one thing but realism another,
and in consequence we set limits to the way you are able to work in our
lives.
Yet time and again you have overturned human expectations,
demonstrating that all things are possible for those who love you.
Teach us, then, to look beyond the obvious and immediate,
and to live rather in the light of your sovereign grace
which is able to do far more than we can ever ask or imagine,
through Jesus Christ our Lord.
Amen.

132

Lord Jesus Christ,
you promise that where two or three are gathered in your name,
you will be there among them.
Help us to trust in that promise –
to know you are here
and to meet with you now through the inner presence of your Holy Spirit.
Open our eyes to your presence,
speak again your word of life,
and help us to listen,
to believe
and to respond.
Amen.

133

Lord Jesus Christ,
thank you for revealing the Father,
not just speaking his word but coming among us,
walking our earth,
sharing our flesh and blood,
to make known his glory,
greatness,
power
and purpose.
Thank you for giving God a human face,
one we can understand and relate to intimately –
making his love real to us.
Draw us closer to you and so closer to him.
Amen.

134

Loving God,
help us, if we would know you better,
to focus our thoughts on Christ,
one with us
yet one also with you.
Amen.

135

Living God,
we do not understand all your ways or know all your thoughts.
There is so much in our lives that troubles and confuses us –
so much hurt and pain we cannot begin to make sense of.
Yet we know that in Jesus you have shared our humanity,
experiencing not just the good in it but the bad.
You understand what it means to be hurt,
to endure suffering,
to face even death itself.
As well as our joys you have shared our sorrows.
Living God,
we thank you for the assurance this gives us –
that whatever we face you will be with us in it.
Amen.

136
Sovereign God,
time and again you have overturned human expectations,
using the most unlikely of people in yet more unlikely surroundings.
You have shown that no situation or person is outside the scope of your
purpose –
that you can use each and every one of us.
Teach us, then, to recognise all you would do among us,
both in our own lives and those of others,
working in ways we would never dare to contemplate or even imagine.
You recognise the potential of everyone and everything –
help us to do the same.
Amen.

Intercession

137
Loving God,
we thank you for the hope you have given us in Christ,
the meaning and purpose,
joy and fulfilment you bring us through him.
Hear now our prayer for those who find it hard to hope,
those for whom life is hard.
Reach out to them in their need,
and may the light of Christ break into their darkness.

We think of those we label as the Third World –
the hungry and undernourished,
homeless and refugees,
sick and suffering –
human beings just as we are,
deprived of their dignity in the desperate struggle for survival.
Reach out to them in their need,
and may the light of Christ break into their darkness.

We think of those who are caught up in war –
overwhelmed by fear and hatred,
their homes and livelihoods destroyed,
each day lived under the threat of violence.
Reach out to them in their need,
and may the light of Christ break into their darkness.

We pray for those who feel overwhelmed by life –
lonely,
frightened,
sad,
weary –
many dreading what the next day might bring.
Reach out to them in their need,
and may the light of Christ break into their darkness.

Loving God,
may the message of hope that Advent brings burst afresh into our world,
bringing help, hope and healing.
And may we, as those who profess the name of Christ,
play our part in showing his love,
displaying his care,
and fulfilling his purpose,
so that he might come again this Christmas to all who have lost hope.
Reach out to them in their need,
and may the light of Christ break into their darkness.
Amen.

138
Loving God,
save us from turning this season of goodwill to all
into one of good things for us,
from indulging ourselves while a world goes hungry.
Help us to celebrate this season with our friends and loved ones,
but also to think of those who have so much less than we do,
those for whom the money we spend on little luxuries would represent a
small fortune
and could make such a difference to their lives.
Open not just our hearts to them but also our hands,
so that they, too, will have cause to rejoice in body as well as in soul.
Amen.

139
Gracious God,
teach us that your coming into the world was not without cost;
that you gave of yourself,
surrendering your life to bring us light.
Help us,
as we celebrate your birth,
to remember also your death
and to be ready in turn to give as well as receive
in the service of your kingdom.
Amen.

Reflective prayer

140
We sang carols, Lord, and offered our worship.
We sent cards and handed out presents.
We ate, drank and made merry,
celebrating,
giving thanks,
rejoicing in another Christmas season.
Only then we saw the scenes on the news,
the report in the paper,
the faces on the poster –
images of drought and famine, hunger and disease:
bellies swollen,
limbs protruding,
eyes glazed over in dull despair,
bodies limp and lifeless –
and we knew that *you* were not rejoicing,
but crying out for help,
calling us to respond from our plenty to their need,
to give to you through giving to them,
to celebrate Christmas by helping others to celebrate life.
How could we forget, Lord?
How could we celebrate the greatest gift ever given in self-indulgence,
extravagance,
greed;
our worship saying one thing,
our lives another;
good news for all turned to good news for us.

Forgive us,
and teach us to make room for both:
to sing carols and offer worship,
to send cards and give presents,
to eat, drink and be merry,
but also to reach out to a world in need
and to respond in love.
Amen.

Closing prayers

141
Lord Jesus Christ,
build your kingdom here on earth.
Lord hear us,
graciously hear us.

Saviour Christ,
rescue your people.
Lord hear us,
graciously hear us.

Light of the world,
scatter our darkness.
Lord hear us,
graciously hear us.

Prince of peace,
heal our wounds.
Lord hear us,
graciously hear us.

Lamb of God,
have mercy upon us.
Lord hear us,
graciously hear us.

Word made flesh,
make us new.
Lord hear us,
graciously hear us.

Emmanuel,
God with us,
come and be with *all*.
Lord hear us,
graciously hear us.
Amen.

142
Whatever the future may hold,
wherever life may lead,
grant, gracious God, that the light of Christ may illuminate our path,
guiding our footsteps and shining upon us,
this day and always.
Amen.

CHRISTMAS

Approach

143
Gracious God,
we come to hear the glorious message of this season,
the glad tidings of great joy,
ever old,
ever new.
We come to recall the faith of Mary,
the commitment of Joseph,
the response of shepherds,
the pilgrimage of wise men,
their experience of that life-changing day in Bethlehem.
Remind us that it is not just their story this season speaks of;
it is ours too!
A Saviour has been born to us who is Christ the Lord:
thanks be to God!

You told Joseph that the words of the prophet would be fulfilled:
that a virgin would conceive and bear a son,
and that he would be called Emmanuel,
meaning 'God is with us'.
Remind us that it was good news not just for one but for all,
and not simply for then but for now.
A Saviour has been born to us who is Christ the Lord:
thanks be to God!

You proclaimed news of great joy to shepherds out in the fields,
the glad tidings that in the city of David a Saviour had been born to us,
the promised Messiah,
the one so long awaited.
Remind us that it was good news not only for them but for everyone,
not just for *that* day but for *every* day.
A Saviour has been born to us who is Christ the Lord:
thanks be to God!

You revealed to John the Apostle the meaning of these great events,
the astonishing truth that you had taken on flesh and blood,
your light, your word, coming into the world,
so that all those who receive him,
who believe in his name,
can be called your children,
children born not of blood,
nor of the will of the flesh,
but of God.

Remind us that it was a promise not confined to the past but for the
present also,
not merely for the chosen few but the whole world.
A Saviour has been born to us who is Christ the Lord:
thanks be to God!

Gracious God,
we thank you for this time,
this season that speaks so powerfully of your love,
that reveals so wonderfully your purpose,
and that demonstrates so clearly your grace.
A time for praise,
a time for joy,
a time for thanksgiving . . .
a time for us!
Remind us that it is not simply a time for some,
but for all.
A Saviour has been born to us who is Christ the Lord:
thanks be to God!
Amen.

144
Almighty God,
like your servant Mary,
we magnify your holy name,
praising you for the gift of Christ
and committing ourselves to your service.
With joyful praise,
we worship you.

Like the shepherds,
we come to meet him,
to celebrate the birth of the Saviour
and respond for ourselves to his coming.
With joyful praise,
we worship you.

Like the magi,
we bow in homage,
seeking to offer our worship,
our gifts,
ourselves.
With joyful praise,
we worship you.

Like your people across the centuries,
we give thanks for this day,
rejoicing that the familiar story that we know and love so well
is able still to speak to our hearts;
that the one who was born among us continues to bring new life to birth.
With joyful praise,
we worship you.

Help us today truly to kneel in heart and mind before the manger
and to marvel at your gift of Christ.
With joyful praise,
we worship you.
Amen.

145
Father God,
we thank you for this day of praise and celebration –
this day on which we set aside time to relive that first Christmas long ago,
on which we remind ourselves of the wonder of the birth of Christ,
on which we remember once more the glad tidings proclaimed to the
shepherds,
witnessed by the wise men,
made possible through Mary.
With joyful hearts,
we come to you.

We come to give thanks for this season –
to rejoice at your great love in sending your Son,
to see for ourselves the truth discovered by the shepherds,
to worship Christ and offer our gifts as wise men came before us.
With joyful hearts,
we come to you.

We come asking you to use us,
just as you used your servant Mary to enter our world.
Take our faith, small though it is,
take our gifts, few though they are,
take our love, poor though this seems,
take our lives, weak though we may be.
With joyful hearts,
we come to you.

Speak to us through this service.
May all we hear draw us closer to you,
all we share remind us of your love,
and so may the message of Christmas come alive in our hearts,
to the glory of your name.
With joyful hearts,
we come to you.
Amen.

146
Gracious God,
through the coming of Christ you have blessed us with the light of your
love:
you have filled our world of darkness with your light,
illuminated our hearts with good news
and made your glory shine upon us so that nothing shall ever overcome it.
In the name of your Son,
Lord, we worship you.

So now we come,
with glad thanksgiving,
with eager expectation,
with heartfelt praise.
In the name of your Son,
Lord, we worship you.

Help us, as we sing your praise and hear your word,
to kneel before the manger in our hearts,
to offer our gifts,
to bring our worship,
to recognise you are with us now.
In the name of your Son,
Lord, we worship you.

So may we go on our way this and every day,
glorifying and praising you for all that we have seen and heard.
In the name of your Son,
Lord, we worship you.
Amen.

147
Loving God,
you have come to us in Christ.
So now we come to you,
to offer our worship,
to hear your word
and to reflect on your love.
Help us through all we share today
to hear the story of Christmas speaking to us as though for the first time.
May familiar and well-loved words take on new meaning,
so that we may share the elation of Mary,
the excitement felt by the shepherds,
and the wonder experienced by the wise men.
May what was news of great joy for *them*,
bring joy likewise to *us*,
this and every day.
Amen.

148
Lord Jesus Christ,
like Mary and Joseph we celebrate your birth,
like the shepherds we would see you for ourselves,
like magi from the East we come to worship,
like countless generations before us
we come to reflect again on the Christmas message,
asking what you would say to us,
and eager in turn to respond to you.
Consecrate the thoughts of our hearts now,
and help us to hear afresh the glad tidings of your coming,
that we may celebrate this season through joyful thanksgiving,
wholehearted service
and sincere devotion.
Amen.

149
Sovereign God,
with Mary and Joseph gazing into the manger,
with shepherds hurrying to and from the stable,
with angels praising you on high,
with wise men kneeling before the Christ-child,
and with generations across the years
who have known and loved your Son,
experiencing his presence in their lives,

so now we join to marvel and celebrate,
offering you our heartfelt worship and joyful praise
for your gift beyond words,
Jesus Christ our Lord.
Amen.

150

Sovereign God,
though we have heard it so many times before,
and though the words of readings and carols we share today
are so familiar we know them almost back to front,
grant that through the worship we bring you
our hearts may thrill again to the good news of Christ,
and our spirits soar at the message of his coming.
Grant us new insights and deeper understanding,
so that our faith may be enriched and our joy increased
as we celebrate the great gift of your Son –
glad tidings yesterday,
today
and every day.
Amen.

151

Lord Jesus Christ,
like the shepherds of old
we come with hearts ablaze to celebrate your birth,
to kneel in wonder,
to offer our thanksgiving
and to respond personally to you.
May we, like them, thrill to the good news of your coming,
and go on our way rejoicing,
making known to those we meet
everything we have found to be true in you.
Amen.

152

God of love,
recalling today how shepherds hurried to Bethlehem,
eager to see for themselves the truth of what they had heard,
so we too are hungry to meet afresh with Christ,
to offer him our worship,
to rejoice in his presence
and to make our personal response to your coming through him.

Direct, then, our thoughts and actions in this time of worship,
so that through our hymns, readings, prayers, reflection and fellowship
we may see and know you better,
appreciating more fully the wonder of this season
and the good news it proclaims for all.
Amen.

Praise

153
Gracious God,
this is a time that means so much to us
and that says so much in so many different ways,
but if there is one thing that stands out above all others,
it is the joy you brought through the birth of Jesus.
A child is born for us,
a son is given –
with joy we greet him!

When Mary learned she was to be the mother of the Saviour she sang out
her praises,
and when Elizabeth greeted her, the baby in *her* womb leapt for joy.
When the multitude of angels appeared to the shepherds,
they proclaimed news of great joy for all people,
and when both shepherds and wise men had seen the Lord for themselves,
they were overwhelmed by the wonder of it all,
going on their way rejoicing.
Time and again it was the same story of spontaneous celebration.
A child is born for us,
a son is given –
with joy we greet him!

Gracious God,
in all the hustle and bustle of Christmas,
the ceremony and tradition with which we surround it,
we can lose sight, sometimes, of the joy at its heart.
We can put so much energy into having a good time,
that we forget what it is we are meant to be celebrating,
being left afterwards with a sense of emptiness,
a feeling that it hasn't been like Christmas at all.
Help us to enjoy all the fun and festivity,
the love and laughter,
the giving and receiving,

but help us also to keep in mind the reality at the heart of this season,
the message that it is finally all about.
A child is born for us,
a son is given –
with joy we greet him!

May the glad tidings of the angels,
the news of great joy for all people,
stir afresh our imagination,
so that we may experience and understand for ourselves the great truth of
Christmas –
that a Saviour is born who is Christ the Lord.
A child is born for us,
a son is given –
with joy we greet him!

Gracious God,
this is a time for rejoicing,
for celebration,
for exulting in your goodness.
We praise and thank you for the wonder of your love
and for the supreme demonstration of that love in Jesus Christ.
A child is born for us,
a son is given –
with joy we greet him!
Amen.

154
Loving God,
at this time of giving and receiving,
of showing our love and gratitude to others through the exchanging of cards
and presents,
we are reminded of the great gift you have given us in Christ
and of how little we have to offer in return.
You have blessed us in so much:
receive our worship.

Whatever we might bring,
it can never repay you.
Whatever we might sacrifice,
it can scarcely begin to express our thanks,
but what we *can* offer and gladly bring is our praise,
our homage,

our adoration,
offered in the name of Jesus.
You have blessed us in so much:
receive our worship.

Like the choir of angels on the night of his birth,
we sing your praise and tell out the good news.
Like the shepherds, returning from the manger,
we give you the glory for all that we have heard and seen.
Like the magi, kneeling in wonder,
we offer our gifts as a token of our love
and sign of our commitment.
You have blessed us in so much:
receive our worship.

Loving God,
at this time of giving and receiving
we do not have much to bring to you,
but we offer this time together –
our songs,
our reading,
our thinking, speaking and listening –
and we offer ourselves, such as we are,
in reverent praise and joyful celebration.
You have blessed us in so much:
receive our worship.
Amen.

155

Lord Jesus Christ,
we know and love the message of Christmas so well,
perhaps too well –
for we have heard and celebrated it so many times
and can assume we have understood all it has to say to us.
Speak afresh,
and help us to listen.

Save us from that danger,
and help us to reflect on what your coming means
for us,
for others,
for all;
for yesterday,

today
and tomorrow.
Speak afresh,
and help us to listen.

Speak to us now,
through readings,
through music,
through prayer,
through your Spirit at work within us.
Speak afresh,
and help us to listen.

Speak through all we shall share together,
nurturing our faith,
strengthening our commitment
and expanding our love for you and for all.
Speak afresh,
and help us to listen.
Amen.

156
Sovereign God,
we can never repay your goodness
and never fully express our thanks,
but we bring you again today our praise and worship,
offered in the name of Jesus.
Joyfully,
we acclaim you.

With angels on the night of the Saviour's birth,
we sing in adoration.
Joyfully,
we acclaim you.

With shepherds,
returning in joy and wonder from the stable,
we praise you for everything we have experienced.
Joyfully,
we acclaim you.

With the magi,
bringing our gifts and bowing in amazement,
we bring you our homage as a demonstration of our love

and expression of our worship.
Joyfully,
we acclaim you.

All we think, say, do and are
we bring to you in reverent praise and joyful celebration.
Joyfully,
we acclaim you.
Amen.

157

Loving God,
we thank you for this day and all it speaks of –
your promise of old to send a Messiah to your people,
the fulfilment of that promise through the sending of your Son,
the realisation of those long years of expectation,
the glad tidings proclaimed by the angels,
the wonder and mystery of that first Christmas.
For all this time means and will always mean,
we praise you.

We thank you for this season's power to move, inspire and challenge,
to gladden the hardest of hearts and most broken of spirits,
to stir our minds and capture our imagination.
For all this time means and will always mean,
we praise you.

We thank you for the special things we associate with Christmas –
the spreading of goodwill,
the sharing of friendship,
the longing for peace,
and the expressing of love.
For all this time means and will always mean,
we praise you.

But above all we thank you for the truth behind this day –
the message that you have come to us,
that you love us,
that you have shared our humanity,
and that you want us to share in your everlasting life,
For all this time means and will always mean,
we praise you.

Loving God,
accept our praise,
receive our thanksgiving,
bless our celebrations,
and may the wonder of the gospel come alive in our hearts this day,
through Jesus Christ our Lord.
Amen.

158
Lord Jesus Christ,
you were born so that you might die.
In awe and wonder,
we worship you.

You took on our humanity
so that you might experience also our mortality.
In awe and wonder,
we worship you.

Only through identifying yourself so totally with us
could you bridge the gap that separates us from God.
In awe and wonder,
we worship you.

You showed us the way of love,
and you followed it through to the end.
In awe and wonder,
we worship you.

You proclaimed forgiveness,
and you paid the price to make it possible.
In awe and wonder,
we worship you.

In life and in death, you testified to the grace of the Father,
and his purpose for all the world.
In awe and wonder,
we worship you.

Help us, as we celebrate again your birth,
never to forget that this was just the beginning of the story.
In awe and wonder,
we worship you.

As we greet you now as the child of Bethlehem,
so let us greet you also as the crucified Saviour
and the risen Lord,
and may we offer you,
this and every day,
our joyful worship
in grateful praise.
In awe and wonder,
we worship you.
Amen.

159
Loving God,
we thank you for this season of Christmas –
for all it has meant to so many over the years,
all it continues to mean to us,
and all it will mean to generations to come.
You have given us so much:
receive our praise.

We thank you for carols old and new,
for familiar and much-loved words of Scripture,
for all that speaks of your coming among us in Christ.
You have given us so much:
receive our praise.

We thank you for reunions with family and friends,
for the spirit of giving and receiving,
for the mood of goodwill and celebration.
You have given us so much:
receive our praise.

We thank you for all the good things we will enjoy –
good food,
good company,
good fun.
You have given us so much,
receive our praise.

Loving God,
help us in all of this to keep sight of the heart of Christmas,
what it all really means –
to celebrate the birth of the infant Christ,
to worship him as joyfully and reverently as shepherds and wise men long ago,

to welcome and follow him as faithfully as those who left everything to be his disciples.
You have given us so much:
receive our praise.

Loving God,
forgive us if we have lost sight of what this season is all about.
Forgive us if we have become over-familiar with its simple yet wonderful message.
Forgive us if we have failed to make room for Christ in our Christmas celebrations.
You have given us so much:
receive our praise.

Speak to us now
through all that we shall do and share,
all we shall sing and hear,
so that our lives may be touched by the wonder of his presence.
You have given us so much,
receive our praise.
Amen.

160

Lord Jesus Christ,
for your coming among us,
your gift of life,
and the peace, joy, hope and love you offer to all,
we worship you.
We praise you that you are still good news,
glad tidings not just for others but for *us*.
With heart and soul,
with all that we are,
together,
we acclaim you.
Amen.

161

Loving God,
we praise you for the new beginning you have brought into our lives,
and the light that continues to guide us.
Teach us to walk in that light day by day,
and so may each moment be a new dawn,
a new beginning,
rich in promise and filled by your love.
Amen.

Confession

162

Lord Jesus Christ,
we recall today how you entered your world
and the world did not know you;
how you came to your own people,
and they would not receive you;
how you were born in Bethlehem,
and there was no room for you in the inn.
From the beginning it was the same old story –
your love rejected,
your grace ignored.
Lord have mercy,
and teach us to receive you with gladness.

We remember that you came to set people free
and to offer a new relationship with God –
breaking down the barriers that keep us apart,
bearing the price of our disobedience,
opening up the way to life.
Yet we remember, too, that though some listened for a moment,
few followed you to the end.
Time and again it was the same old story –
your love rejected,
your grace ignored.
Lord have mercy,
and teach us to receive you with gladness.

We know we are no better,
each of us guilty, day after day, of spurning your guidance,
forgetting your goodness
and abandoning your way.
We talk of commitment,
but our faith is weak;
we speak of following you,
but follow only our own inclinations;
we claim to be a new creation,
but it is the old self that still holds sway.
Time and again it is the same old story –
your love rejected,
your grace ignored.
Lord have mercy,
and teach us to receive you with gladness.

Lord Jesus Christ,
we marvel that, despite it all –
the world's hostility and our own faithlessness –
still you reach out in love,
never giving up,
refusing to write us off.
We thank you that you are always ready to offer a fresh start,
a new beginning,
to anyone willing to receive it.
Come what may, it is the same old story –
you continue seeking us out,
however often we thrust you aside,
your love rejected,
your grace ignored.
Lord have mercy,
and teach us to receive you with gladness.
Amen.

163
Forgive us, Lord,
for we struggle to grasp the wonder of your love,
the miracle of what you have done in Christ.
Lord, hear us,
graciously hear us.

We lose sight of the reality that you lived and died among us,
walking our earth,
sharing our humanity.
Lord, hear us,
graciously hear us.

We forget that the stable at Bethlehem was the start of something
that would change history for ever,
its impact still reverberating around the world today.
Lord, hear us,
graciously hear us.

We fail to understand the way you can work in our lives,
how small beginnings can yield unexpected results
out of all proportion to our faith.
Lord, hear us,
graciously hear us.

Speak again now of all you have *done*,
are doing
and *will do*,
and help us to celebrate with body, mind and soul
the priceless blessing of your gift in Christ.
Lord, hear us,
graciously hear us.
Amen.

164
Gracious God,
we thank you that you have given us good news in Christ,
a message that has thrilled generations across the years,
uplifting,
encouraging,
challenging
and renewing.
Fill us, Lord,
and thrill us afresh.

We thank you for the way that message has spoken to us,
shown to be glad tidings in so many ways.
Yet we confess that we sometimes lose our initial sense of awe and wonder,
and no longer feel the urge to respond to your love as powerfully as we once
did.
Fill us, Lord,
and thrill us afresh.

Forgive us for becoming casual and complacent in our faith,
failing to make time to worship,
and forgetting the need to nurture our relationship with you.
Fill us, Lord,
and thrill us afresh.

Speak to us again,
meet us through the living Christ,
and open our hearts to the renewing touch of your Holy Spirit.
So may we catch again the sense of urgency felt by the shepherds
as they rushed to Bethlehem,
and may the wonder of your love burn within us each day,
to your glory.
Fill us, Lord,
and thrill us afresh.
Amen.

165
Lord Jesus Christ,
we remember today how you came to our world
and found no welcome;
how, from the very beginning,
you were shut out,
no room for you even in the inn.
Have mercy, Lord,
on us, and on all.

Forgive us that we are sometimes guilty of shutting you out in turn,
failing to make room for you in so many areas of our lives.
Despite our words of faith and commitment,
we turn our back on you when we would rather not face your challenge.
Have mercy, Lord,
on us, and on all.

Forgive us,
and help us to make room for you,
not just this Christmas but always.
Teach us to give you not merely a token place in our hearts,
but to put you at the very centre of our lives.
Have mercy, Lord,
on us, and on all.

Come now,
and make your home within us,
by your grace.
Amen.

166
How much time, Lord, will we make for you this Christmas?
How much time, before, during and after the celebrations,
to reflect on your love?
Will we put you at the centre of our celebrations,
the heart of our lives,
or relegate you to the margins,
include you almost as an afterthought?
Forgive us, for all too often,
at Christmas or otherwise,
we have time for just about everything . . .
except *you.*
Amen.

167
Forgive us, Lord,
for we fail to reflect on our lives,
to weigh them in the balance,
ensuring we've got things right.
We become casual,
complacent,
accepting the status quo with barely a second thought.
Whatever else we do this season,
teach us to make room for the things that really matter;
room,
above all,
for you.
Amen.

168
Forgive us, Lord,
for we know this season so well,
its message being so familiar that it no longer moves us,
no longer speaks as it once did.
Help us to see beyond the festive trappings and traditions
to the awesome truth they proclaim:
your Word,
your Son,
your love,
your gift –
good news,
now and always.
Amen.

169
Loving God,
remind us again that you are a God of grace,
reaching out to the bad as well as the good,
to sinners as well as saints.
Teach us that you chose Mary,
representative of the powerless;
shepherds,
examples of the socially marginalised;
and countless others across the years whom society had rejected.
Help us, then, to turn to you,
acknowledging our faults and weaknesses,

knowing that, despite them all,
you have a place for us in your kingdom,
through Jesus Christ our Lord.
Amen.

170
Merciful God,
forgive us,
for we mistake the material trappings of this season for the real thing,
confusing show with substance,
ornament with essence.
Help us to see beyond the glitz to the true meaning of Christmas.
Amen.

171
Living God,
forgive our over-familiarity with the wonder of your love
and help us still to celebrate the good news of Christ –
something to go on getting excited about,
day after day.
Amen.

172
Lord Jesus Christ,
we recall that you came to our world,
to your people,
yet among so many found no welcome.
From the very beginning the majority shut you out,
and of those who did accept you
many did so only half-heartedly.
Forgive us that sometimes we do the same.
Help us to make room for you,
and to give you not just a token place,
but one at the very centre of our lives.
Amen.

Thanksgiving

173

Loving God,
we remember today the birth of Jesus Christ –
your gift to humankind,
your coming among us as flesh and blood,
your honouring of age-old promises spoken through the prophets.
The Word became flesh and dwelt among us,
full of grace and truth:
thanks be to God!

We do not remember those promises alone,
but so many others associated with this time –
your promise to Mary that she would bear a son,
to Simeon that he would not taste death before seeing the Messiah,
and, above all, your promise to anyone who receives Christ and believes in
his name
that they will become your children,
born not of human will,
but through your gracious purpose
sharing in your eternal life.
The Word became flesh and dwelt among us,
full of grace and truth:
thanks be to God!

Loving God,
we praise you that all you promised to do was wonderfully fulfilled in
Christ,
that through him your faithfulness was most marvellously demonstrated;
the ultimate proof of your love and mercy.
We praise you for the reminder this Christmas season brings
that you are a God we can always depend on,
one in whom we can put our trust, though all else fails.
The Word became flesh and dwelt among us,
full of grace and truth:
thanks be to God!

So now we look forward in confidence to the ultimate fulfilment of your
word,
that day when Christ will be acclaimed as King of kings and Lord of lords.
Until then, we will trust in you,
secure in your love,
confident in your eternal purpose,
assured that, in the fullness of time, your will shall be done.

The Word became flesh and dwelt among us,
full of grace and truth:
thanks be to God!
Amen.

174
Loving God,
we thank you for the great truth we celebrate at Christmas,
the fact that, in Christ, your light shines in the darkness
and that nothing has ever been able to overcome it.
Despite hostility and rejection,
the combined forces of hatred and evil,
still the radiance of your love continues to reach out.
The people that walked in darkness have seen a great light:
thanks be to God!

We thank you for the light that dawned in the life of Zechariah and
Elizabeth,
that transformed the future for Mary and Joseph,
and that lit up the sky on the night of the Saviour's birth.
The people that walked in darkness have seen a great light:
thanks be to God!

We thank you for the light that flooded into the lives of shepherds,
that guided wise men on their journey to greet the new-born king
and that answered the prayers of Simeon and Anna.
Always you are with us,
in life or in death leading us through the shadows.
The people that walked in darkness have seen a great light:
thanks be to God!

We thank you for the light you brought through the life and ministry of
Jesus –
freedom for the captives,
sight to the blind,
healing for the sick,
comfort to the broken-hearted,
peace after confusion,
acceptance after condemnation,
hope after despair,
joy after sorrow.
The people that walked in darkness have seen a great light:
thanks be to God!

We thank you for the light that illuminates our lives today
and that leads us step by step on our journey through life –
the lamp of your word,
the beacon of prayer,
the glow of fellowship,
the tongues of fire of your Holy Spirit,
and the living reality of Jesus by our sides,
the dawn from on high.
The people that walked in darkness have seen a great light:
thanks be to God!

Loving God,
you came to our world in Christ, bringing life and light for all.
Shine now in our hearts
and may the flame of faith burn brightly within us,
so that we, in turn, may bring light to others,
and, in so doing, bring glory to you.
The people that walked in darkness have seen a great light:
thanks be to God!
Amen.

175
Loving God,
we come today to remember with gratitude the birth of your Son.
Lord,
we thank you.

We remember how prophets foretold his coming,
and how those words were wonderfully fulfilled in Bethlehem.
Lord,
we thank you.

We remember how you needed Mary to bring him into the world,
and how she willingly allowed you to work through her.
Lord,
we thank you.

We remember how shepherds heard the good news,
and how, having seen the truth of it for themselves,
they went on their way rejoicing.
Lord,
we thank you.

We remember how Simeon held you in his arms,
and with praise in his heart gave thanks to you.
Lord,
we thank you.

We remember how generations since have seen your face revealed in Christ,
and through him heard you speaking in a new way.
Lord,
we thank you.

We remember the past
so that we might discover you in the present
and find faith for the future.
Lord,
we thank you.

Be born in our hearts today
that we may be born again to eternal life.
Amen.

176

Gracious God,
we thank you for the joy of Christmas-time:
the joy you gave to Mary, shepherds and magi as you entered the world in Christ;
the joy you have brought to generations across the centuries as they have come to faith;
the joy you offer us now in a living and saving knowledge of Jesus Christ.
For the wonder of this season,
gratefully we rejoice.

We thank you that, whatever we face, you are with us through him,
supporting us by your love,
enriching us by your grace,
equipping us through your Spirit.
For the wonder of this season,
gratefully we rejoice.

Inspire us afresh each day with the good news of Christ
and the reality of his presence in our hearts,
so that we may go on our way exulting,
now and always.
For the wonder of this season,
gratefully we rejoice.
Amen.

177
Thank you, Lord, for your love,
constantly reaching out though we fail to appreciate all you've given
or how much it cost you.
Thank you that your blessing and goodness is not dependent on our
deserving,
but goes on being poured out day after day,
generous beyond measure.
Amen.

178
Gracious God,
thank you for the closeness you have made possible through your Son,
not just with others
but above all with you.
Thank you for the relationship we can enjoy with you
through your coming among us in Christ,
sharing our humanity and dying our death to bring us life.
Help us to celebrate the love at the heart of this season
and, through him,
draw us closer to you each day.
Amen.

179
Lord of all,
thank you for the message of Christmas,
so familiar and well loved
yet still able to surprise us with joy,
causing us to catch our breath in wonder.
Amen.

Petition

180
Gracious God,
we thank you today for your extraordinary gift of Christ
and all that it points to –
the wonder of your love,
the extent of your love
and the constancy of your purpose.
And we thank you for the most extraordinary thing of all:
that you came in Christ not simply to a few but to all –

to good and bad, saints and sinners,
to ordinary, everyday people like us.
You reached out and accepted us as we are:
teach us to accept others in turn.

We thank you that you chose Mary,
representative of the powerless,
to be the one to bear your Son;
that you chose shepherds,
examples of the socially marginalised,
to be the first to hear the good news;
that you chose Bethlehem,
symbol of the least and lowest,
to be the place where you were born.
Through the manner of your coming among us,
and through the life you lived in Christ,
you repeatedly overturned this world's values and expectations,
demonstrating your special care for the poor,
the needy,
the weak
and the humble –
all those ready to admit their dependence on you
and seek your help.
You reached out and accepted us as we are:
teach us to accept others in turn.

We do not find it easy to accept others,
for we are biased towards the attractive and the successful,
taken in by appearances,
blind to the reality beneath the surface.
Our attitudes are shaped by deep-rooted prejudices and preconceptions
that make us wary,
suspicious,
even hostile towards those who do not conform to our flawed expectations.
We jump to conclusions that all too often say more about ourselves than
anyone.
Though we claim it is wrong to judge,
in our hearts we not only judge but also condemn.
Forgive us, and remind us of the example of Christ
whom the so-called righteous repeatedly condemned for associating with
the unacceptable.
You reached out and accepted us as we are:
teach us to accept others in turn.

Gracious God,
you have a place in your heart not just for the few but for all,
not only for the good but for the unlovely,
the undesirable,
the undeserving.
You look deep into the hearts of all,
and where we see ugliness, you see someone infinitely precious,
so valuable that you were willing to endure death on a cross to draw them to
yourself.
Help us to recognise that no one,
no matter who they are,
is outside the breadth of your love or the scope of your mercy.
You reached out and accepted us as we are:
teach us to accept others in turn.
Amen.

181
Gracious God,
there are so many lessons we can learn from this season,
but none more important than that shown to us by Mary.
After the events leading up to the birth of Jesus –
the shock,
the excitement,
the uncertainty,
the celebration –
we read that she 'treasured all these words
and pondered them in her heart'.
While shepherds made their way home
exulting in all they had seen and heard,
she made time to stop
and think
and take stock;
time to reflect on what it all might mean
for herself
and others.
You come still,
you speak still:
teach us to make space to listen,
to understand
and to respond.

We remember how Jesus, in turn, throughout his ministry,
made time for you –
time amid all the pressures and demands to be still in your presence,

to discern your will,
and to understand his calling.
He went into the wilderness,
he drew aside from the crowds,
he agonised alone in Gethsemane,
giving *you* the opportunity to speak,
and *himself* the opportunity to hear your voice.
You come still,
you speak still:
teach us to make space to listen,
to understand
and to respond.

We are not good at making such time to reflect,
so easily becoming caught up in the fervour of the moment
or bogged down in the routine of life.
We flit from this to that,
pursuing now this goal, now another,
our lives long on activity but short on substance.
Deep down we are scared of looking inwards,
afraid of the hollowness we might see there,
the emptiness that might be exposed.
Yet until we are ready to be honest,
both with ourselves and with you,
true peace and fulfilment will always elude us.
You come still,
you speak still:
teach us to make space to listen,
to understand
and to respond.

Gracious God,
teach us this Christmas-time,
like Mary, to ponder all that you have said and done;
to listen again to familiar readings and carols,
to hear again the story we know so well,
but to consider what it all might mean,
what you are saying not just to others but also to us.
In all the celebrations and rejoicing,
the praise and the worship,
help us to be still before you,
so that our lives may be opened to your living Word,
your renewing love
and your redeeming power.

You come still,
you speak still:
teach us to make space to listen,
to understand
and to respond.
Amen.

182
Lord Jesus Christ,
we celebrate today your birth in Bethlehem –
a birth that changed the course of history for ever.
We rejoice that the future of the world was shaped by your coming,
irreversibly transformed by your life, death and resurrection.
A new chapter had begun:
help us, in turn, to start again.

We remember how you brought a new beginning to so many –
not just to Mary and Joseph on the night of your birth,
but to countless others throughout your ministry
and to innumerable generations since,
offering the opportunity to put their mistakes behind them,
to let go of the past and embrace the future,
secure in your forgiveness,
transformed by your grace.
A new chapter had begun:
help us, in turn, to start again.

So we come now, this Christmas-time,
acknowledging our faults and repeated disobedience.
We come recognising our need for help
and our dependence on your mercy.
We come to hear the good news of your birth,
the glad tidings of the dawn of your kingdom,
and, in the light of that message,
to seek your renewing touch upon our lives.
A new chapter had begun:
help us, in turn, to start again.

Lord Jesus Christ,
we have no claim on your love,
no reason to expect your goodness,
for we fail you day after day, week after week.
Yet we celebrate today the glorious truth that you came into our world,

you lived among us,
you died our death,
and you rose again, victorious over sin and death!
A new chapter had begun:
help us, in turn, to start again.
Amen.

183
Almighty and loving God,
we come together on this day
to celebrate the birth of your Son,
the child laid in a manger,
our Lord and Saviour Jesus Christ.
You have done great things for us,
and we are glad.

We come recalling that first Christmas centuries ago;
the message proclaimed by the angels –
news of great joy!
You have done great things for us,
and we are glad.

We come remembering the faith of Mary,
the thanksgiving of the shepherds,
and the worship of the wise men.
You have done great things for us,
and we are glad.

We come reminding ourselves of your great love shown to us and all people
through your coming and sharing our humanity,
through your living and dying among us.
You have done great things for us,
and we are glad.

Loving God,
we thank you for this time of year –
its mood of joy and celebration,
its spirit of goodwill and desire to work for peace,
the renewing of old friendships
and the coming together of families,
the lessons and carols that we know and love so well.
You have done great things for us,
and we are glad.

Save us, Lord, from becoming over-familiar with this season,
from ever imagining we know all there is to know about it,
or presuming we have understood all there is to understand.
You have done great things for us,
and we are glad.

Teach us to listen for your voice and look for your presence,
to hear your call and respond to your guidance.
You have done great things for us,
and we are glad.

May we, like Mary, have the faith to believe that with you nothing is
impossible;
like the shepherds to go in heart and mind even to Bethlehem
to see what you have done;
like the wise men to offer you our worship
and present to you our gifts;
like the great company of angels
to sing glad and joyful songs of praise.
You have done great things for us,
and we are glad.

So may we, when the festivities are over and Christmas is past,
return to our daily lives glorifying and praising you for all we have seen and
heard,
the wonder of your love revealed in Christ!
You have done great things for us,
and we are glad.

Praise be to you, now and for ever!
Amen.

184
Gracious God,
at this time of giving,
help us to offer the worship,
thanksgiving,
service
and witness
that you alone deserve.
Lord, hear us,
graciously hear us.

At this time of receiving,
help us to open our hearts to your gift of Christ,
making his love and life our own.
Lord, hear us,
graciously hear us.

At this time of joy,
help us to celebrate the good news at its heart,
the wonder of your coming in Christ,
walking our earth and sharing our humanity.
Lord, hear us,
graciously hear us.

At this time of sharing,
help us to reach out to those whose hearts are heavy,
crushed by hunger,
poverty,
sorrow
and pain.
Lord, hear us,
graciously hear us.

At this *special* time,
open our lives to your transforming power,
your love that is able to make all things new.
Lord, hear us,
graciously hear us.

Take what we are,
and direct what we shall become,
through Jesus Christ our Lord.
Amen.

185
Lord Jesus Christ,
we remember today that those who first heard the good news were not the
religious elite
or those respected in the eyes of the world,
but shepherds –
ordinary, everyday people like us.
Just as we are, Lord,
take us and use us.

We remember how, throughout your ministry,
you welcomed those whom society had little time for,
who were counted as nothing;
those who would have known their need
and made no presumption on your goodness.
Just as we are, Lord,
take us and use us.

Teach us, through their experience, that, whoever we are,
however insignificant we may feel,
you value us for who we are,
accept us despite our faults,
and love us come what may.
Just as we are, Lord,
take us and use us.

May the knowledge of how much we matter to you be good news for us,
this and every day.
Amen.

186
Lord Jesus Christ,
help us to make room for you in our lives,
not at the margins,
allowed in when it suits us,
but at the heart of everything we think, say and do,
so that your guidance may direct our steps,
your purpose restore our hope,
your mercy renew our faith
and your love fashion our being.
Whatever else we allow to be squeezed out of life
teach us to welcome you afresh into our hearts,
today and every day.
Amen.

187
Lord Jesus Christ,
help us to keep the message of your birth, life,
death and resurrection
close to our hearts,
and, through reflecting on what all that means,
to stay as close to you
as you are to us.
Amen.

188

Lord Jesus Christ,
born in a stable,
be born in us today.
Help us to make room for you in our hearts,
to kneel before you,
and to hear afresh the good news of your coming among us,
your living and dying for all.
Amen.

189

Almighty God,
help us at this season, to go in heart and mind to Bethlehem –
to the stable,
the manger,
the baby in the straw –
so that your Son,
our Saviour,
may be born again,
in *us*.
Amen.

190

Living God,
despite the glitz, bustle, hype and expense,
Christmas proves a let-down for many,
promising much yet delivering little.
Awaken the hearts of all to the glorious surprise at its heart –
the wonder of your Son,
born in a stable and laid in a manger,
your Word made flesh and love incarnate –
a gift beyond price that will never disappoint.
Amen.

191

Loving God,
help us to remember that whatever we receive this Christmas,
it can never compare with that greatest gift of all:
your coming among us in Christ.
Amen.

192
Almighty God,
in the rush and bustle of this season,
with so much to remember
and such a lot to do,
teach us to make time simply to pause
and to ponder what it all means.
Amen.

193
Living God,
keep alive the magic of this season,
an awareness of the mystery at its heart.
Though we lose our childish illusions,
may we retain a youthful sense of wonder at your coming among us in
Christ.
Amen.

194
Sovereign God,
open our hearts to the radiance of your love,
the light that shone in the birth of your Son
and that continues to shine today,
nothing being able to overcome it.
Help us to glimpse afresh the true romance of this season,
the full wonder and beauty of it all,
able to shed light in our hearts not just at Christmas
but each moment of every day.
Amen.

195
Loving God,
remind us that after the stable came a cross,
after birth, death,
after celebration, sacrifice,
and after pleasure, pain,
each expressing a single theme:
the wonder of your love.
Help us to rejoice in all that this season means,
not just in part
but in full.
Amen.

196

Teach us, Lord God,
amid the festivity and merriment of this season,
to delve deeper,
discovering what's of real value within it:
the new life you offer through your Son,
bringing nourishment to body, mind and soul.
Help us to receive for ourselves that most precious gift of all.
Amen.

197

Almighty God,
teach us to put you at the centre of Christmas,
so that you can transform our lives –
the things we do,
the way we think,
the people we are,
each being touched by your presence
and made new by your love.
Amen.

198

Through this Christmas season, Lord,
as we wrap and unwrap our presents,
teach us what it means to give and receive –
to open our hearts not just to loved ones,
but to others and to you.
Amen.

199

Whatever else we grow out of, Lord,
help us to keep faith in you,
who alone gives meaning not just to Christmas,
but to all.
Amen.

200

May the faith we profess in you, Lord,
be as real today as it was yesterday,
as vibrant every day as it is on Christmas Day.
Amen.

201

Gracious God,
help us not just to *hear* the message of Christ's birth
but to make it our own,
meeting him afresh,
responding to his grace
and welcoming him into our lives.
May we recognise more fully what he means for us and for all –
what you accomplished through his life, death and resurrection,
and what you continue to accomplish in countless human hearts.
Grant that the child of Bethlehem –
the crucified Saviour and risen Lord –
may be born in us today,
and that we may walk with him to our journey's end.
Amen.

202

Gracious God,
we have heard countless times the story of your coming in Christ,
perhaps so often that it fails to speak as it once did.
We hear the words,
sing the carols,
listen to the message,
without really taking it in,
familiarity blunting its force.
Help us to hear it again today as though for the first time,
to take ourselves back in heart and mind to Bethlehem
and to the events surrounding the birth of your Son,
so that you may speak to us afresh,
just as you spoke then,
making known the immensity of your love
and your gracious purpose for all,
made flesh through Jesus Christ our Lord.
Amen.

203

Loving God,
though we can never begin to dispel this world's darkness,
help us to do whatever we can,
however insignificant it may seem,
to help lessen it a little.
Amen.

204
Living God,
like Anna and Simeon before us,
may our hearts leap for joy as we celebrate your coming in Christ,
the one anticipated for so long
and on whom the hopes of so many rested.
Help us to recognise in him the fulfilment of your promises
and answer to our needs;
the one who brings an unsettling challenge yet also offers peace;
who brings light and life not only to us but to all the world.
Teach us to respond faithfully,
offering our grateful praise,
and witnessing in word and deed
to everything you have done through him.
Amen.

205
Loving Lord,
keep alive in us the hopefulness of youth,
that same sense of joy in simple things
and expectation for the future.
Though life dishes out knocks and disappointments,
help us to carry on believing in what you hold in store –
wonderful beyond words.
Amen.

206
Living God,
teach us that the joyful message proclaimed at Bethlehem all those years ago
is good news for us today,
here and now.
Amen.

207
Lord Jesus,
child in the manger,
man on the cross,
risen Saviour,
Lord of all,
be born in us today.
Amen.

208
Gracious God,
help us to learn from the example of Mary.
Teach us this Christmas-time
to ponder, as she did, all that you have said and done:
to listen again to familiar readings and carols,
and to hear again the story we know so well,
but also to consider what it all might mean;
what you are saying not just to others but also to us.
Amid all the celebrations and rejoicing,
help us to be still before you
so that we may open our hearts to your living word,
your renewing love
and your redeeming power,
and so know the presence of Jesus within us.
Amen.

209
Loving God,
remind us that in taking flesh and being born as a baby,
you identified yourself fully with humankind,
not imposing yourself upon us
but drawing alongside,
inviting a response.
Remind us that you made yourself vulnerable,
exposing yourself to persecution and rejection from the beginning,
willingly bearing the price of love.
Open our hearts today to respond –
freely, gladly and reverently –
ready to risk something for you
who risked so much for us.
Amen.

210
Loving God,
you have given us and all the world
good news in Christ.
Help us to hear it afresh each day,
recognising it as news for *us*.
Help us to receive it with both our minds and our hearts,
always looking to understand more of what it continues to say.
And help us to share what Christ has done for us
so that others in turn may celebrate what he has done for them.
Amen.

211
Loving God,
challenge us through the example of the shepherds.
Teach us that it is not enough simply to accept the claims of others,
but that we need to experience the truth of the gospel for ourselves.
Help us, then, to open our souls to the presence of Christ,
and to welcome him into our lives.
Help us to know the reality of his Spirit at work within us,
and to accept the good news,
not just with our heads but also with our hearts.
Amen.

212
Loving God,
as the years go by and life drifts on,
sometimes we find it hard to keep faith alive.
As we face life's repeated disappointments,
as prayer after prayer seems to go unanswered,
so faith falters,
the dreams of youth dulled by the reality of experience.
Yet you tell us through Jesus never to stop looking forward,
never to stop believing in the future.
Lord Jesus Christ, help us to go on trusting in the victory of your love
and the coming of your kingdom
despite everything that seems to deny it.
Amen.

Intercession

213
Lord Jesus Christ,
born an outcast and refugee,
in weakness and frailty,
as we rejoice today,
hear our prayers for all those who have no cause for celebration.
Lord, in your mercy,
hear our prayer.

We pray for the hungry and the homeless,
the poor and the unemployed,
the oppressed and the exploited,
the lonely and the downhearted.
Lord, in your mercy,
hear our prayer.

We pray for the sick and the dying,
the sorrowful and the bereaved,
victims of violence and war,
all whose lives have been shattered by tragedy and disaster.
Lord, in your mercy,
hear our prayer.

Lord Jesus Christ,
born to set your people free,
come again to our world,
bringing reconciliation where there is division,
and comfort where there is sorrow,
hope where there is despair,
and confidence where there is confusion.
Lord, in your mercy,
hear our prayer.

Come and bring light where there is darkness,
and love where there is hatred,
faith where there is doubt,
and life where there is death.
Lord, in your mercy,
hear our prayer.

Lord Jesus Christ,
come again to our world,
and bring that day nearer when your kingdom will come,
and your will be done.
Lord, in your mercy,
hear our prayer.
Amen.

214
Lord Jesus Christ,
you came to our world,
but there was no place for you.
You came to your own people,
but they were not ready to receive you.
You were born in Bethlehem,
but there was no room for you in the inn.
You walked among us, sharing our humanity,
but had no place to rest your head.
You returned to your home town,
but were without honour in your own country.

You came to bring life to all,
but you were put to death on a cross.
You know what it is to be homeless,
hungry, abandoned, rejected,
and so we bring you our prayers
for all those who endure such need today.
Friend of the friendless,
hear our prayer.

We pray for those who have no roof over their head
or no place to call their own –
waiting perhaps on council housing lists,
or evicted because they cannot pay the rent,
homes destroyed by natural disaster,
or left behind as they flee from persecution or the threat of war.
Friend of the friendless,
hear our prayer.

We pray for those who live in poor and overcrowded conditions,
in shanty towns, or refugee camps,
hostels, or bed-and-breakfast accommodation,
tenement blocks, or run-down slums;
for those who sleep rough on the streets.
Friend of the friendless,
hear our prayer.

And we pray too for those who feel they have no place in society –
the unemployed,
the poor,
the lonely,
the oppressed,
the persecuted,
the terminally ill.
Friend of the friendless,
hear our prayer.

Lord Jesus Christ,
reach out to all who face such situations.
Grant the assurance that you care,
courage to believe in the future,
and strength to meet the present.
Friend of the friendless,
hear our prayer.

Grant your help to those who offer help,
your support to those who campaign for justice,
your blessing to all who seek to bring hope where there is only hopelessness.
Friend of the friendless,
hear our prayer.

May we, with them, make real your love,
and show your compassion,
working together for your kingdom.
Friend of the friendless,
hear our prayer.
Amen.

215
Living God,
we thank you for the great message of the gospel,
the glad tidings of your love,
the good news of your coming to our world through your Son.
May that message inspire us again this Christmas-time
and in the days to come.
Speak your word of love,
and move in the hearts of all who hear it.

We thank you that the good news of Christ has challenged people across the
ages,
and that though it has been proclaimed countless times,
though we have heard it ourselves so many times before,
it continues to be news for us and for all –
able still to speak to individuals across the world
and change their lives.
Speak your word of love,
and move in the hearts of all who hear it.

So now we pray for those you have specially called to proclaim the good
news –
ministers,
preachers,
evangelists,
teachers –
all with the special gift and responsibility of communicating your word.
Grant them wisdom,
dedication,
inspiration,

and courage,
that they may faithfully witness to you in the power of the Holy Spirit.
Speak your word of love,
and move in the hearts of all who hear it.

We pray also for those who hear the good news,
responding in different ways –
those who have closed their minds to what you would say to them –
may your love break through the barriers they erect;
those who have heard but failed to understand –
may their hearts be opened to the truth;
those who have yet to grasp that the gospel is good news for them –
may the experience of meeting Christ transform their lives;
those who have responded and come to faith –
may their knowledge of you continue to grow.
Speak your word of love,
and move in the hearts of all who hear it.

Finally we pray for those who long for good news,
who cry out for glad tidings –
the poor, starving, sick and lonely,
the oppressed, persecuted, unloved, bereaved –
so many people across the world who despair of ever seeing hope rekindled.
May the message of the gospel mean good news for them.
Speak your word of love,
and move in the hearts of all who hear it.

Living God,
come again to your world this Christmas-time,
through your word,
your Spirit,
your people,
and the living presence of Christ,
and so may the message of the gospel truly be good news for all people.
Speak your word of love,
and move in the hearts of all who hear it.
Amen.

216
Lord of all,
we have heard again the good news of Jesus Christ,
the glad tidings of his coming,
and we have rejoiced in the wonder of this season.

But we pray now for those for whom it brings no joy,
serving only to remind them of their pain.
Come again to your world,
and turn tears into laughter,
sorrow into gladness.

We pray for the poor, the hungry, the homeless –
those for whom this Christmas will simply be another day in the struggle for
survival;
for those caught up in war, violence and persecution –
those for whom this Christmas might be their last;
for the unloved, the lonely, the homeless –
those for whom Christmas merely heightens their sense of isolation.
Come again to your world,
and turn tears into laughter,
sorrow into gladness.

We pray for the anxious, the troubled and the fearful –
those for whom Christmas will be swamped by worries;
for the sick, the suffering, the broken in body and mind –
those for whom this Christmas means only another day of pain;
and we pray for the bereaved, the divorced, the estranged –
those for whom Christmas brings home the memory of happier times.
Come again to your world,
and turn tears into laughter,
sorrow into gladness.

Lord of all,
you give us a vision through the song of Mary of the way the world ought
to be
and one day will be:
a world in which you show the strength of your arm
and scatter the proud,
in which you bring down the powerful
and lift up the lowly,
in which you fill the hungry with good things
and send the rich away empty;
a world of justice,
in which good will triumph,
evil be ended
and the meek inherit the earth.
Give us confidence to believe that day can come
and the resolve to make it happen.
Stir the hearts of your people everywhere to work for change –

to bring the dawn of your kingdom closer
and so translate that vision into reality.
Come again to your world,
and turn tears into laughter,
sorrow into gladness.
Amen.

217
Gracious God,
we say that it is more blessed to give than to receive
but in practice we rarely give any indication of believing that.
We claim that Christmas is a time for giving as well as receiving,
but our gifts are usually reserved for family and friends,
the chosen few.
Gratefully, we remember today that your gift of Christ is so very different –
good news *for* all,
the Saviour *of* all,
given *to* all.
God of grace, you have given us so much:
teach us to give in return.

We thank you that you offered yourself freely,
not for any reward, save that of sharing your love,
and you gave everything,
even life itself,
so that anyone and everyone might come to know your goodness,
irrespective of creed, colour or culture.
God of grace, you have given us so much:
teach us to give in return.

We pray now for your world in all its need –
those in lands racked by poverty,
crushed by debt,
overwhelmed by famine or natural disaster.
God of grace, you have given us so much:
teach us to give in return.

We remember those who are persecuted,
denied justice,
or falsely imprisoned.
God of grace, you have given us so much:
teach us to give in return.

We remember those whose lands are torn by hatred,
scarred by violence,
broken by war.
God of grace, you have given us so much:
teach us to give in return.

We remember those afflicted by sickness,
struggling with disability,
or crushed by suffering.
God of grace, you have given us so much:
teach us to give in return.

We remember those overcome by depression, bereavement or broken
relationships,
all for whom the present brings trouble
and the future seems uncertain.
God of grace, you have given us so much:
teach us to give in return.

Gracious God,
at this time of giving and receiving
reach out in love to your aching world.
Bring comfort in distress,
courage in adversity,
confidence in uncertainty
and compassion in suffering.
Strengthen all those who work to build a fairer society
and a more just world,
and challenge each of us, who have so much,
to share from our plenty with those who have so little.
May we not just talk in this season about goodwill to all,
but do something to show what it means.
God of grace, you have given us so much:
teach us to give in return.
Amen.

218
God of love,
we pray for all who will be celebrating Christmas this year,
enjoying presents, parties, food and fun,
yet not having heard or accepted or understood what Christmas is all about.
Speak to them now,
and help them to respond.

We pray for those who have never heard the gospel,
or who have received a distorted picture of its message,
or who have failed to recognise it is good news for them.
Speak to them now,
and help them to respond.

We pray for those who have closed their hearts and minds to Christ,
refusing to listen or consider further,
rejecting your Son as so many rejected him at his coming.
Speak to them now,
and help them to respond.

We pray for those who have come to faith
but barely realised what that means,
seeing perhaps just a small part of all you have done,
or seeking to know more but troubled by doubts and questions.
Speak to them now,
and help them to respond.

God of love,
come again to our world this Christmas,
breaking through our cosy traditions,
our narrow horizons,
our neatly packaged celebrations.
Speak to *us* now,
and help *us* to respond.

Help us and all people to glimpse the wonder of your awesome love –
a love revealed in the Christ who came and lived among us,
who suffered and died on the cross,
who rose and reigns with you,
and who will come again to draw all things to himself.
Speak to *us* now,
and help *us* to respond.
Amen.

219
Loving God,
we praise you for all we have to rejoice in at Christmas,
this special reminder year by year of your coming to us in Christ.
Come to us now,
and help us to keep you at the centre of our celebrations.
Lord, in your mercy,
hear our prayer.

Come to our loved ones,
our families,
our friends,
all those we hold dear,
all those of whom we will think over these coming days.
Help us as we celebrate and make merry
to think also of Christ,
and through drawing closer to him
to grow closer together.
Lord, in your mercy,
hear our prayer.

Come to those in special need –
the poor, the sick, the lonely and sad,
the homeless, the helpless,
the oppressed and persecuted;
all those for whom life is hard and the future seems bleak.
Reach out to them in love,
and give them something to celebrate.
Lord, in your mercy,
hear our prayer.

Loving God,
may the light of Christ break into the lives of people everywhere,
bringing your joy,
your peace,
your hope,
and your love,
a song of praise on their lips,
and celebration in their hearts.
Lord, in your mercy,
hear our prayer.

Come to them,
come to us,
come to all,
and send us on our way,
rejoicing in the gospel,
and praising you for the wonder of your grace.
Lord, in your mercy,
hear our prayer.
Amen.

220
Lord of all,
we pray for all who worship you today,
all across the world who rejoice in the good news of the birth of Jesus.
Speak your word of life,
and be born in our hearts today.

May the reading of Scripture,
the singing of carols,
the offering of prayers,
and the sharing of fellowship,
convey something of the wonder of your love.
Speak your word of life,
and be born in our hearts today.

May the faith of all your people be enriched,
and the life of the Church renewed,
by the presence of the living Christ,
so that the gospel may be proclaimed through its joyful witness,
and the glad tidings of your coming in Christ bring new hope,
joy,
meaning
and purpose
to the lives of all.
Speak your word of life,
and be born in our hearts today.

Lord of all,
reach out to your Church and to people everywhere at this glad time of year,
touching our lives with the living presence of Christ.
Speak your word of life,
and be born in our hearts today.
Amen.

221
Lord Jesus Christ,
born in Bethlehem,
come afresh to our world today –
to our towns and cities,
our fractured communities,
our divided nations,
our bleeding planet.
Son of God,
hear us.

Lord Jesus,
born in a stable,
come afresh to the poor and homeless,
the disenfranchised,
the weak and vulnerable,
the outcast, oppressed and exploited.
Son of God,
hear us.

Lord Jesus,
born to suffer and die,
come afresh to those who are sick,
those in pain,
those facing death,
those who mourn loved ones.
Son of God,
hear us.

Lord Jesus Christ,
born in ages past,
be born in *us* today.
Amen.

222
Living God,
save us from frittering away our money at Christmas on trivia,
while a world goes hungry;
from turning this season of goodwill to *all* into one of good things for *us*.
Teach us to make room in our celebrations for those who,
in this life,
have so little to celebrate
and to give as generously to them as we have so richly received.
Amen.

223
For too many, Lord, this season proves to be a let-down,
approached with anticipation yet ultimately disappointing,
like a cheap Christmas cracker.
Speak afresh to our world,
so that instead of concentrating on trivia that promises much yet delivers little,
people may learn to focus on Christ,
the one who gives meaning not just to this time of year,
but to time itself.
Amen.

224

At this time of family get-togethers, Lord,
open our eyes to the wider family of the Church
and of all people across the world.
May Christmas truly be a time of coming together;
a time when,
remembering the One made flesh,
we grow together,
united in your love,
and celebrating our common humanity,
barriers broken and divisions overcome.
Amen.

225

Redeemer God,
for so many people Christmas stirs a sense of your presence,
reminding them of a reality beyond this world,
a relationship they crave,
and for a few days churches bulge at the seams
as carols are sung
and the gospel message is given a hearing . . .
but then January sales beckon,
calling the multitude back to their true devotion,
and you are forgotten again for another year.
Break through the trappings of this season
and touch human hearts the world over,
so that instead of being just briefly remembered,
you may be known and loved,
this and every day.
Amen.

226

Gracious God,
at this time of giving and receiving,
help us to share the message of your love –
a gift not just for us but for all.
Whatever things we keep to ourselves,
may the good news of your coming not be among them.
Amen.

Reflective prayers

227
What does it mean, Lord:
all this hustle and bustle,
buying and spending?
Why have we spent these last few weeks chasing our tails,
rushing here, there and everywhere,
sending cards,
wrapping presents,
buying food,
singing carols?
We enjoy these –
each in their way being a part of the Christmas we've grown to know and
love –
but occasionally it all seems just that bit too frenetic:
so much to be done
yet uncertainty as to why we do it.
We *do* know, Lord, of course we do,
only we can't help being distracted,
the truth at the heart of this season –
the gift of your love –
being crowded out by other matters,
each seeming so pressing at the time
yet ultimately of such little concern.
Forgive us, Lord, for thinking of everything and everyone …
except you,
for focusing on so much trivia …
and losing sight or what really counts.
Teach us to celebrate all that is good in this season,
but also to distinguish the froth from the substance,
the wrapping from the gift,
the gold from the glitter.
Teach us to step back,
to pause,
and to ponder,
so that may we find meaning not just in today
but in every day,
not just at Christmas
but always.
Amen.

228

Well, that's it for another year, Lord.
It's all over, bar the shouting:
the presents opened,
the food eaten,
the festivities winding down –
back soon to the old routine.
It's been good,
memorable in its way,
yet we can't help feeling something's been missing –
as though we've overlooked a vital detail,
the most important job left undone.
That's it –
we see it now:
we've made time for feasting and fun,
for family and friends,
but we haven't made time for you,
to worship you as you deserve.
We've given you *some* time, of course,
more than usual, in fact,
sharing in all kinds of services to mark this festive season,
but they were as much about our edification as your glory,
about following tradition as following Christ.
We sang songs we've sung so often before,
and barely considered their meaning.
We've listened to words we've heard year after year,
but scarcely taken them in.
We offered prayer,
but no longer expected you to hear your voice.
Forgive us,
and remind us again of what Christmas is all about.
Break through the wrapping and trimmings,
the box into which we so neatly package you,
and help us again to see your love
in the child in a manger,
in the man on a cross,
in the risen, ascended Lord.
So may we offer our worship not as an afterthought,
but as our first concern,
an instinctive spontaneous response,
offered to your praise and glory.
Amen.

229

Laid to sleep in rustic manger,
born into a world of danger,
one with us, yet deemed a stranger –
Christ be born again.

Where a world lies bruised and broken,
words of hate are cruelly spoken,
fear and hate is daily woken –
Christ be born again.

Where a multitude needs feeding,
where the poor for help are pleading,
where the refugee lies bleeding –
Christ be born again.

Where the sorrowful are sighing,
where the weak and sick are dying,
where the crushed at heart are crying –
Christ be born again.

Jesus born in humble stable,
come and end at last our Babel;
you alone, our Lord, are able –
Christ be born again.

230

Lord Jesus, at your coming,
The angels joined in praise,
They danced in celebration,
They set the sky ablaze,
They brought the world glad tidings,
The news that you had come,
That you were born in Bethlehem –
God's one and only son.

Lord Jesus at your coming,
your mother sang aloud,
for you would bless the humble,
and overthrow the proud.
She knew you'd free the captives,
and reach out to the poor;
bring justice, hope and dignity –
fulfilment of the Law.

Lord Jesus at your coming,
the shepherds rushed to see;
the question each was asking,
'Can these things really be?'
They crowded round the manger,
and, sheltered from the cold,
found Jesus wrapped in swaddling clothes,
just as the angels told.

Lord Jesus, at your coming,
the wise men knelt with joy
and offered you their worship,
though you were just a boy.
They brought you gifts so costly –
gold, frankincense and myrrh –
portending what you came to do,
and everything you were.

Lord Jesus, at your coming,
you turned the world around,
you gave our life new meaning,
as multitudes have found.
You broke the hold of evil,
and opened wide the door
to peace and lasting happiness,
and life for evermore.

Closing prayers

231
Gracious God,
we have heard the good news of this season,
the glad tidings of the birth of your Son,
our Saviour, Jesus Christ,
and we have rejoiced in everything which that means.
Yet we know that this message is not just for us but for everyone –
your love being for all the world,
your concern for all people,
your purpose without limits.
Help us then to go now with joy in our hearts
and wonder in our eyes,
to share the love that you have shown,
and to make known the great thing that you have done in Christ.
May Jesus be born again in our hearts
and made known through our lives.

Through the words we say and the deeds we do,
the love we share and the compassion we show,
the faith we proclaim and the people we are,
may his light shine afresh in the world,
bringing hope, healing, joy and renewal.
Grant that all may come to know you for themselves,
and so celebrate the news of great joy:
your coming among us in Christ to bring us life in all its fullness.
May Jesus be born again in our hearts
and made known through our lives.

In his name we go,
to live and work for him,
with joyful thanks and grateful praise.
Amen.

232
Almighty God,
we have heard once more the wonderful message of your coming to us in
Christ –
tidings of great joy,
good news for all people.
As you have come to us,
so may we go for you.

We thank you for that message,
the well-loved words we have heard and sung again today –
so familiar,
so often repeated,
yet still so special and meaningful.
As you have come to us,
so may we go for you.

We thank you for the faith and trust of Mary –
her willingness to accept your will;
for the pilgrimage and gifts of the wise men –
their determination to seek and respond;
for the simple actions of the shepherds –
their hearing the message and seeing its truth for themselves,
then sharing with others what they had experienced!
As you have come to us,
so may we go for you.

Teach us, we pray, as we celebrate this Christmas-time,
to learn from their example,
to follow in their footsteps,
to share their faith.
As you have come to us,
so may we go for you.

Teach us to know the reality of Christ born for *us*,
and in our turn to pass on what we have discovered through him to those
around us.
As you have come to us,
so may we go for you.
Amen.

233
Loving God,
thank you for the message we have been reminded of again:
the glad tidings of your coming to us in Christ.
Live in us,
that we may live for you.

Once more we have rejoiced in the fulfilment of your word,
the ancient promises of Scripture.
Live in us,
that we may live for you.

Once more we have celebrated, like shepherds and wise men long ago,
the birth of your Son,
our Saviour.
Live in us,
that we may live for you.

Speak to us afresh through all we have heard and shared,
so that we, with them,
may go on our way rejoicing,
knowing the reality of your love for ourselves,
and offering our service to Christ in grateful praise and heartfelt worship.
Live in us,
that we may live for you.
Amen.

234

As those who walked in darkness saw a great light,
as shepherds glimpsed the heavenly host,
as wise men saw the star
and as generations of believers have witnessed your glory –
full of grace and truth –
so, Lord God, may the brightness of your presence fill our lives,
enriching, inspiring, leading and illuminating,
this and every day.
Amen.

235

Loving God,
grant that the faith we profess might be as real tomorrow and every day as it
is now.
Grant that, when Christmas is over,
the good news at its heart will continue to shape our life
and that we will continue to offer the one at its centre our wholehearted
discipleship.
Amen.

Christingle prayers

236

Lord Jesus Christ,
giver of life and bringer of hope,
meet with us as we gather before you.
Shine in our hearts,
light up our minds
and sparkle in our souls,
so that something of your radiance may be seen in us,
testifying to your grace and goodness,
and leading others to glimpse your glory
Flood our lives with the brilliance of your love,
so that it may glow not just *in* us
but *through* us,
a light set upon a hill
bringing glory to you.
Amen.

237

Living God,
at this glad season
open our hearts and minds to what it is all about:
your coming to our world
and sharing our humanity in Christ
so that we might share in your eternal kingdom,
rejoicing in the blessings you delight to shower upon us.
Speak through this simple service
that the symbols of Christingle and story of the Christ-child
may help us to glimpse also the Lord of life
and Light of the world,
finding in him *our* Lord
and *our* Light,
with us this day and always.
Amen.

238

Loving God,
for the light you bring to our lives in countless ways –
everything that enriches, enthrals, inspires and fulfils,
we praise you.
For the light you have brought in Christ,
shining into the darkness of our world
and bringing peace, hope, compassion and forgiveness,
we thank you.
Open our hearts and minds to your presence here,
so that we may receive more fully everything you long to give us,
and rejoice each day in the light of your love.
Amen.

239

Lord Jesus Christ,
be born in us today,
such that the flame of our Christingles may burn brightly our hearts,
and the light of your love shine in and through our lives.
Amen.

240

In the darkest places, Lord,
and the darkest moments of life,
shine your light of love and goodness,

peace and joy,
so that, whatever obscures it,
it will finally win through.
Amen.

241
Light of Christ,
fill our hearts.
Light of Christ,
direct our path.
Light of Christ,
brighten our days.
Light of Christ,
shine in our darkness.
Light of Christ,
transform our lives.
Amen.

242
Almighty God,
we yearn for a day when your will is done
and your kingdom come,
when your light bathes all in its radiance
and there is an end to sorrow and suffering,
darkness and death,
but we believe also that you care about us here and now,
about life today as much as life to come.
So we pray,
come among us.

Reach out into the shadows of pain and sickness,
poverty and hunger,
evil and injustice,
ignorance and bigotry,
hatred and violence,
tragedy and bereavement –
all that holds people captive,
denying the life and light you long to give them.
Overcome with love all that undermines happiness and dignity,
and help us, wherever possible, to do the same,
doing all we can to bring you kingdom closer on earth
as it is in heaven.

So we pray,
come among us.
In the name of Christ.
Amen.

243
Lord Jesus Christ,
reach out through your Spirit
and bring light to whose lives are shadowed by trouble and turmoil:
the shadow of famine and starvation,
trauma and catastrophe,
sickness and pain,
anxiety and fear,
loneliness and rejection,
hatred and violence,
death and bereavement.
Though the shadows may lengthen
and the darkness deepen,
may your light finally break through
and shine for evermore.
Amen.

244
Living Lord,
light to the nations,
light of our lives,
shine, we pray, into our world today,
banishing all that obscures your goodness
or obstructs your will.
Amen.

245
The light of Christ illuminate your path
and fill your days with sunshine.
The light of Christ shine in your darkness
and banish the clouds.
The light of Christ radiate *to* you and *through* you,
to the glory of his name.
Amen.

EPIPHANY

Approach

246
Lord Jesus Christ,
we celebrate today how wise men were prepared to seek,
and keep on seeking,
persevering despite setbacks and disappointments
until they found you.
We remember how you promised that all who seek will find,
that those who ask will receive,
that to those who knock the door will be opened;
and so we come now,
asking for your guidance and seeking to know you better,
so that, drawing ever closer to you,
we may offer our love and our lives in glad response,
to the glory of your name.
Amen.

247
Sovereign God,
we are here in the name of Christ.
Meet with us
and speak to us now,
through him.
Be a light to our path
and a lamp to our way.

Reveal to us more of his way:
what it means to know, love and serve him,
what he shows us of you,
what he has done for us all
and what he continues to do in our world.
Be a light to our path
and a lamp to our way.

Remind us of the new beginnings he makes possible,
his transforming love that takes what is
and determines what shall be.
Be a light to our path
and a lamp to our way.

Teach us more of his kingdom in which the last will be first
and the least greatest,
your will done here on earth as it is in heaven.
Be a light to our path
and a lamp to our way.

Speak of how your word,
your promises
and your Law
find fulfilment in him;
and of how he took on himself the punishment that was rightfully ours,
sharing both our life and our death.
Be a light to our path
and a lamp to our way.

Sovereign God,
open our hearts,
and help us to glimpse something more of your light, love, grace and truth,
made known in him.
Be a light to our path
and a lamp to our way.
Amen.

248
Gracious God,
illuminate our minds as we come to worship you.
Reveal to us afresh the wonder of your presence,
intensity of your love,
scope of your mercy
and extent of your purpose.
Open our hearts to know you better,
and to see your hand at work around us.
Speak now through this time of worship
and every day through the presence of your Spirit,
the fellowship of your people
and the riches of your word,
so that our lives may reflect the radiance of Christ,
the light of life.
Amen.

249
Light of life,
Light of the world,
come among us as we meet together
and flood our lives with the brightness you alone can bring.
So fill us that we may shine in turn for you,
our words and deeds testifying to your love for all
and enlightening the lives of others.
Flow *within* us
and *through* us,
to the glory of your name.
Amen.

Praise

250
Everlasting God,
we celebrate your coming to our world in Jesus Christ,
your light that continues to shine in the darkness of our world.
We praise you for the way your love shone in so many lives during his
ministry;
through the healing he brought to the sick,
comfort to the distressed,
promise to the poor,
and forgiveness to the lost.
Receive our worship,
and shine in our lives today.

We praise you for the light that has shone in so many lives since,
the faith you have nurtured in innumerable hearts;
new beginnings,
new purpose,
new life born within them.
Receive our worship,
and shine in our lives today.

We rejoice that you are at work in our lives here and now,
inviting us to bring our hopes, fears and concerns before you
in the knowledge that you will always meet our needs,
no situation being beyond your power to transform and redeem.
Receive our worship,
and shine in our lives today.

We praise you for the assurance that evil will be overcome;
that hope will replace despair,
joy come after sorrow,
and life triumph over death –
that even the deepest darkness will be turned to light!
Receive our worship,
and shine in our lives today.

Fill us now with the light of Christ.
May it illuminate our worship and guide our footsteps,
so that we may live as a lamp for others,
to the glory of your name.
Receive our worship,
and shine in our lives today.
Amen.

251
We remember today that, from the beginning,
the good news of Jesus Christ was not just for a few,
but for all.
Loving God,
receive our praise.

You made it known to shepherds tending their flocks by night,
ordinary, everyday people pursuing their daily life and work,
unlikely yet special representatives of your chosen nation.
Loving God,
receive our praise.

But you made it known also to wise men from the East,
strangers living far away,
with no knowledge of you,
and regarded by many at the time as having no part in your promises.
Loving God,
receive our praise.

For the message behind this –
that there is no one outside your love,
that the message of the gospel transcends all barriers,
that you want to bring light to all corners of the world –
Loving God,
receive our praise.

For the fact that we are part of your great purpose –
heirs of the promise made to Abraham,
members of the great company of your people,
called to proclaim the gospel to those around us –
Loving God,
receive our praise.

For the knowledge that your light continues to shine –
despite opposition,
persecution,
and rejection by so many –
Loving God,
receive our praise.

For the way so many have followed the example of Jesus
and responded to your call –
through the waters of baptism,
through commitment to your Church,
through a life of faith and witness –
Loving God,
receive our praise.

You have made your light shine in our hearts.
Help us to show our gratitude
by walking in the path it illuminates,
and shedding that light on those around us.
Loving God,
receive our praise.
Amen.

252
Sovereign God,
we are reminded today of the journey of the magi:
of how they stepped out into the unknown,
persevering despite adversity,
searching diligently until their quest was rewarded.
Lead us in turn, Lord,
and help us to find.

We come today, seeking as they did:
looking to learn from their experience,
to worship the one before whom they knelt in homage,
to understand what his birth, life, death and resurrection mean for us.
Lead us in turn, Lord,
and help us to find.

Help us to discover each day a little more of your love,
and to discern more of your gracious purpose,
so that we may offer our lives to you,
in joyful praise
and glad thanksgiving.
Lead us in turn, Lord,
and help us to find.
Amen.

253
Lord Jesus Christ,
Light of the World,
you shine in our hearts,
banishing all that obscures your goodness
and darkens our lives.
Shine now,
shine always.

Illuminate this time of worship,
so that in every part it will draw us closer to you,
revealing more of your purpose
and unfolding more of your grace.
Shine now,
shine always.

Come to us
as we come now to you,
and flood our lives with the radiance of your love
so that it may shine not just *in* us
but also *through* us –
a light set upon a hill
bringing glory to you.
Shine now,
shine always.
Amen.

254
Lord Jesus Christ,
hope of your people,
hope of your world,
touch now our lives as we gather before you.
Shine in our hearts,
illuminate our minds

and light up our spirits,
so that we will grasp more clearly the hope you give us:
the assurance of your love
and the joy of life in all its fullness,
giving you praise and worship,
here, now, and for all eternity.
Amen.

Confession

255
Lord Jesus Christ,
this is a time that reminds us of the journey of the wise men –
their determination to greet you that inspired them to persevere
despite difficulties and disappointments along the way.
Forgive us that we lack their sense of vision,
their willingness to undertake a pilgrimage into the unknown
in the confidence that you will lead us.
Forgive us if our response to you has lost its initial sparkle,
the flame that once burned so brightly within us now grown cold
and our hearts no longer stirred by the prospect of seeing you face to face.
Lord, in your mercy,
hear our prayer.

This is a day that reminds us of how you led the magi on their journey,
your light always with them –
a guiding star,
a sign of your presence,
a call to follow until they came to the place where the child lay.
Forgive us that we are so often closed to your guidance,
unable or unwilling to see your hand,
more concerned with our own way than yours,
reluctant to commit ourselves to anything when the final goal is not clear.
Forgive us for talking of faith as a journey
but turning it instead into a comfortable destination.
Lord, in your mercy,
hear our prayer.

This is a day that reminds us of the magi's worship –
their falling to their knees before you,
their bowing in homage,
their mood of joy and exultation, wonder and privilege.

Forgive us for losing such feelings –
for being casual,
complacent,
even blasé when we come into your presence,
taking it all for granted.
Forgive us for offering our worship out of habit or duty,
outwardly correct but inwardly empty.
Lord, in your mercy,
hear our prayer.

This is a day that reminds us of the magi's gifts,
their presents of gold, frankincense and myrrh,
each one an expression of love,
a token of esteem,
a symbol of all you meant to them.
Forgive us that, though we have received so much,
we give so little,
our thoughts being more for ourselves than for you,
our offering a routine rather than a sacred act of consecration.
Forgive us that we give what we feel we can afford
rather than what your great love and goodness deserves.
Lord, in your mercy,
hear our prayer.

Lord Jesus Christ,
we come to recommit ourselves to the journey of faith,
to follow where you would lead,
to bring you our worship
and to offer ourselves in joyful service.
Receive us in all our weakness
and go with us on our way,
so that we may live and work for your kingdom.
Lord, in your mercy,
hear our prayer.
Amen.

256
Loving God,
you guided the wise men to Bethlehem,
offering a light for their path,
and in faith they responded.
Forgive us that all too often we fall short of their example.
Gracious Lord,
have mercy.

You offer us guidance in innumerable ways –
through the light of your word,
the illumination of your Holy Spirit,
the fellowship of your Church,
and the encounter of prayer,
yet so often we either fail to hear or refuse to see.
Gracious Lord,
have mercy.

We are too preoccupied with our own small affairs,
eyes only for the immediate moment,
our vision impeded by trivial concerns,
so we fail to recognise where you are leading us.
Gracious Lord,
have mercy.

We believe we know just where we are going,
just what we want from life,
and exactly how we can get it,
and we resist any suggestion that we need to think again.
Gracious Lord,
have mercy.

Loving God,
forgive us our foolishness,
our stubbornness,
our weakness.
Gracious Lord,
have mercy.

Forgive our pride,
our lack of faith,
our closed minds.
Gracious Lord,
have mercy.

Forgive us for ignoring your guidance,
resisting your will,
and as a result so often walking in darkness.
Gracious Lord,
have mercy.

Meet with us again we ask,
and may the light of your love shine in our hearts,
so that we cannot fail to respond in grateful praise and joyful service.
Gracious Lord,
have mercy.
Amen.

257
Great and glorious God,
forgive us, for we repeatedly obscure your light,
stopping it from both shining in or out.
Pull back the curtains we close against you,
so that the light of your love
and radiance of your presence
may flood *into* our hearts
and *out* through our lives.
Amen.

Thanksgiving

258
For the light of each new day,
Lord of all,
we thank you.

For the light of the sun,
warming and sustaining,
Lord of all,
we thank you.

For the light of love,
gladdening and enriching our lives in so many ways,
Lord of all,
we thank you.

For the light of truth,
combating evil, injustice, falsehood and corruption,
Lord of all,
we thank you.

For the light of goodness and compassion,
deeds great and small contributing to heal and help,
restore and renew,
Lord of all,
we thank you.

For the light of wisdom,
instructing and equipping for life,
Lord of all,
we thank you.

For the light of Christ,
shining across history,
across the world,
and into our hearts,
Lord of all,
we thank you.

For the light we have received,
that is with us now,
and that lies in store in your eternal kingdom,
Lord of all,
we thank you.
Amen.

259
Thank you, Lord, for the new day you bring through the rising of your Son –
the new beginnings,
new life,
you daily make possible through him.
Thank you for your promise that,
however deep the darkness may seem,
light will dawn again,
shining in our hearts for evermore.
Amen.

260
Thank you, Lord, for your light,
guiding to Bethlehem,
shining on the mountain,
pouring from the empty tomb
and sparkling in our hearts.
Thank you for the knowledge that,
whatever life brings,
you will give light to our path,
this and every day.
Amen.

Petition

261
God of love,
we remember today, on this Epiphany Sunday,
how wise men from the East came seeking the new-born king,
how finally they reached the end of their journey,
and how they knelt in worship before the infant Jesus.
Help us to learn from their example.
Guide our footsteps,
and lead us closer to Christ.

Teach us to continue faithfully on the path you set before us,
remembering that true faith involves a journey of discovery
as well as arrival at a destination.
Guide our footsteps,
and lead us closer to Christ.

Teach us to seek your will resolutely,
even when the way ahead is not clear.
Guide our footsteps,
and lead us closer to Christ.

Teach us to look at the world around us,
and to recognise the signs through which you might be speaking to us.
Guide our footsteps,
and lead us closer to Christ.

Teach us to keep on trusting in your purpose,
even when the response of others may give us cause for doubt.
Guide our footsteps,
and lead us closer to Christ.

Teach us to offer to Jesus our wholehearted devotion –
not simply our gifts but our whole lives,
given to him in joyful worship and grateful praise.
Guide our footsteps,
and lead us closer to Christ.
Amen.

262
Lord Jesus Christ,
as magi came to your light,
walking in faith to their journey's end,

help us to follow in turn,
your grace and truth offering a lamp to our path.
Shine in our hearts, Lord,
and help us to know you better.

As John the Baptist greeted you as the Lamb of God,
sent to take away the sins of the world,
may we too welcome you,
joyfully receiving the forgiveness you so freely offer.
Shine in our hearts, Lord,
and help us to know you better.

As the disciples responded to your call,
leaving their nets and fishing instead for people,
so may we consecrate ourselves to your service,
seeking in word and deed to walk your way and testify to your saving grace.
Shine in our hearts, Lord,
and help us to know you better.

As the multitude thronged around you,
eager to listen to your word and witness your mighty deeds,
may we also hunger to hear your voice and comprehend your glory –
to experience first-hand the wonder of your love.
Shine in our hearts, Lord,
and help us to know you better.
Amen.

263
Almighty God,
thank you for making yourself known to us in Christ.
You are above and beyond us,
defying definition,
and yet you took flesh and entered our world,
revealing yourself in human form.
Lighten our path,
and lead us in your way.

Help us to glimpse your glory –
to discern your power,
experience your love,
receive your mercy
and know your peace.
Lighten our path,
and lead us in your way.

Illuminate our lives with the light of your love,
shining *on* us,
in us
and *through* us,
by the grace of your Son,
our Lord Jesus Christ.
Lighten our path,
and lead us in your way.
Amen.

264
Gracious God,
such is your love for us that you go on calling,
however long it takes for us to respond,
and you go on leading,
however tortuous our journey of faith may be.
Lighten our path
and guide our footsteps.

We may put off a decision,
keep you at arm's length –
still you are there to guide,
striving to draw us to yourself.
Lighten our path
and guide our footsteps.

We may encounter obstacles that impede our progress,
that lead us astray or that obscure the truth,
yet always you are there to set us back on the way.
Lighten our path
and guide our footsteps.

Teach us that your love will never let us go,
and so help us to make our response
and to bring our lives to you in joyful homage,
knowing that you will continue to lead us until our journey's end.
Lighten our path
and guide our footsteps.
Amen.

265

Living God,
you have brought light to our lives,
illuminating each day with your love.
Shine in and through us,
so that we may help to bring a little light in turn to others.
Amen.

266

Lord Jesus Christ,
Light of the world,
shine *on* us,
shine *in* us,
shine *through* us,
and so bring honour to your name.
Amen.

267

Lord Jesus Christ,
light a torch in our hearts,
a fire in our eyes,
a flame in our hearts,
a candle in our lives
and a beacon in our world.
Shine on us,
in us
and through us,
to your glory.
Amen.

268

God of life,
may the promise of the sunrise be echoed in our minds,
the warmth of the midday sun flow into our hearts
and the peace of the sunset touch our souls;
and, when life seems dark,
teach us to remember that still you are with us
and that we will again see your light.
Amen.

269
Eternal God,
when life seems a puzzle
and faith itself can make no sense of it,
lead us forward out of darkness into light,
out of confusion into certainty,
out of the storm into tranquillity.
Put our minds at rest and our spirits at peace,
through Jesus Christ our Lord.
Amen.

270
God of light,
be with us in our darkness,
until night passes and your light breaks through.
Amen.

271
Gracious God,
even when all seems dark,
teach us that your light will continue to shine.
Amen.

272
Lord Jesus Christ,
like the wise men following your birth,
teach us to search for you until we come to faith,
and then to go on searching just as eagerly and whole-heartedly
to discover more of your will and purpose for our lives.
Continue to surprise us with the wonder of your love
and the awesomeness of your grace,
so that we may know and love you better each day.
Amen.

273
Lord Jesus Christ,
you have told us to seek and we shall find.
Yet that search is not always easy.
As we look for meaning in our lives,
there is so much that puzzles and perplexes.

The more we discover,
the more we realise how little we have understood.
Give us the determination of the wise men to keep on looking,
despite all that obscures you,
until at last we find our perseverance rewarded
and, glimpsing your glory,
we kneel before you in joyful worship.
Amen.

274
Almighty God,
in the darkest moments of life,
the darkest places,
the darkest experiences,
bring your love,
your life,
your light.
Amen.

275
Gracious God,
remind us again as we worship you of how much you love us
and how much you are willing to do for our sakes.
Teach us to appreciate the full extent of your devotion
and to respond by consecrating our lives to Christ,
so that his grace may flow through us,
leading us out of darkness into his marvellous light.
Shine upon us,
within us
and through us,
and make us new.
Amen.

276
Sovereign God,
without your light in our lives we walk in darkness,
denied the joy, peace, hope, strength and guidance you alone can give.
So we ask, through your grace,
that the light of Christ might break yet more fully into our hearts
and shine more brightly through our lives,
to your glory.
Amen.

277
Lord Jesus Christ,
come among us
and kindle a flame in the hearts of your children here and everywhere,
that, by your grace, we may all become a little more like you,
to the glory of your name.
Amen.

278
Living God,
teach us today that though life may sometimes seem dark
and your light but a memory,
always you are there,
able to turn sorrow into dancing,
our tears to laughter.
Remind us afresh of the good things you desire for us,
the joy, peace and blessing you would have us enjoy,
and speak also of the way you will see us through,
however deep the shadows,
until that day when we live in the light of your love for evermore,
through Jesus Christ our Lord.
Amen.

279
Lord Jesus Christ,
open our souls to your grace,
our minds to your strength,
our hearts to your love
and our lives to your light.
Draw us ever closer to you and live within us,
so that your goodness and compassion may shine through,
helping to brighten the lives of those around us
and, above all, pointing to you.
Amen.

Intercession

280
Lord Jesus Christ,
you promised that those who seek will find,
and in the pilgrimage of the magi we find proof of that promise.
So now we bring you our prayers for all in our world,
known and unknown to us,
who, in different ways, are searching.
May your light shine upon them:
a beacon of hope and a lamp to their path.

We pray for those who search for meaning,
their lives empty,
devoid of purpose,
hungry for something or someone to put their trust in.
In the bewildering variety of this world's voices,
each claiming to offer the answer,
may your love break through
and the message of the gospel touch their hearts,
so that they might find in you
the one who is the way, the truth and the life.
May your light shine upon them:
a beacon of hope and a lamp to their path.

We pray for those for whom the journey of life is hard,
beset by pain, sickness and sorrow,
or overwhelmed by disaster, deprivation and injustice.
In the trials they face and the burdens they struggle with
may your love break through
and the message of the gospel bring strength and comfort,
help, healing and inspiration.
May your light shine in the darkness:
a beacon of hope and a lamp to their path.

We pray for those unsure of the way ahead,
faced by difficult choices and vital decisions,
troubled by situations in which they can see no way forward
or doubting their ability to cope with the demands the future will bring.
In the uncertainties of this ever-changing world,
may your love break through
and the message of the gospel bring a new sense of direction,
an inner peace,
and the assurance that you alone can give,

so that, whatever they may face,
they will know that nothing will ever separate them from your love.
May your light shine upon them:
a beacon of hope and a lamp to their path.

We pray for those who have gone astray –
betraying their principles,
or their loved ones,
or, above all, you.
In this world of so many subtle yet powerful temptations,
may your love break through
and the message of the gospel bring new beginnings,
so that, however low they may have fallen,
they will know themselves forgiven,
accepted
and restored.
May your light shine in the darkness:
a beacon of hope and a lamp to their path.

Lord Jesus Christ,
hear our prayer
for all who seek purpose, help, guidance and mercy.
May they find in you the answer to their prayer
and the end to their searching.
Amen.

281
Lord of Light,
we have remembered today the journey of the wise men –
how, inspired by what they took to be a sign,
they set off in search of a new-born king,
a king who would change not simply their lives,
nor merely the life of his people,
but the life of the world.
Come again now,
and may light shine in the darkness.

We remember how they persevered in their quest,
travelling in faith
even though they had no clear idea of where they were heading,
or any certainty of what they would find when they reached their
destination.
Come again now,
and may light shine in the darkness.

We remember how they refused to be discouraged,
despite their reception in Jerusalem,
despite the fact that no one seemed to have any idea that a new king had
been born.
Come again now,
and may light shine in the darkness.

We remember how they kept going,
single-minded in pursuit of their goal,
until at last their determination was rewarded
and they came face to face with the infant Jesus.
Come again now,
and may light shine in the darkness.

Living God,
we pray for all who seek today,
all those who are looking for a sense of purpose in their lives,
all who are searching for spiritual fulfilment,
all who long to find you for themselves.
Come again now,
and may light shine in the darkness.

Help them to keep looking,
even when the journey is demanding
and no end seems in sight;
to keep believing,
even when others seem oblivious to their quest
or scornful of it;
to keep on trusting,
even when those they look to for guidance
seem as confused and as lost as they are.
Come again now,
and may light shine in the darkness.

Living God,
you have promised through Jesus Christ that those who seek shall find.
May the experience of the wise men inspire all who seek for truth to keep on
searching,
in the assurance that they too,
come what may,
will one day complete their quest
and discover you for themselves.
Come again now,
and may light shine in the darkness.
Amen.

282

In the darkness of sorrow and despair, Lord,
bring light.

In the darkness of war and hatred, Lord,
bring light.

In the darkness of pain and suffering, Lord,
bring light.

In the darkness of fear and superstition, Lord,
bring light.

In the darkness of poverty and need, Lord,
bring light.

In the darkness of famine and starvation, Lord,
bring light.

In the darkness of injustice and exploitation, Lord,
bring light.

In the darkness of death and loss, Lord,
bring light.

In every place and experience of darkness, Lord,
bring light.
Amen.

283

Lord Jesus Christ,
shine into the darkness of this world,
into its suffering and sorrow,
evil and injustice.
Lord, hear us,
graciously hear us.

Brighten the lives of those who wrestle with illness, pain and infirmity;
those who mourn loved ones or face the prospect of their passing;
those who are poor, homeless or hungry;
those who are oppressed and exploited;
those who are depressed, troubled or weary.
Lord, hear us,
graciously hear us.

Shine into the hearts of those who do not know you,
those who reject you,
ignoring, rejecting or even opposing your way.
Lord, hear us,
graciously hear us.

Illuminate our own path,
opening our hearts each day to the radiance of your love and blessing.
Come through your Spirit and shed your light afresh upon all.
Lord, hear us,
graciously hear us.
Amen.

284

Lord Jesus Christ,
come among us now,
for so often we look around and see only darkness –
a shadow over our lives,
denying hope and destroying life.
Come again now,
and may your light shine on all.

Come into our hearts,
our homes,
our country,
our world,
and shine upon us,
so that we might bathe in the glow of your love
and the radiance of your grace,
your light scattering the darkness for ever.
Come again now,
and may your light shine on all.
Amen.

285

Saviour Christ,
shine in the darkness of our world –
into our sorrow,
hurt,
pain
and despair.
Bathe us, Lord,
in the sunshine of your love.

Scatter the clouds that hang over us –
the shadows of hatred,
violence
and war.
Bathe us, Lord,
in the sunshine of your love.

Break into the night-time of evil and injustice,
and bring among us a new dawn.
Bathe us, Lord,
in the sunshine of your love.

Illuminate the way of all who cry out for a lamp to their feet and light to
their path.
Bathe us, Lord,
in the sunshine of your love.
Amen.

286
In a beautiful but broken world,
full of so much good yet so much evil,
so much joy yet so much sorrow,
we bring you, Lord, our prayers for others.

Where hardship has crushed the spirit,
poverty, injustice or disease having destroyed faith in the future,
Lord Jesus Christ,
may your love bring light.

Where war and suffering scar your world,
hatred, greed and intolerance erupting into violence,
Lord Jesus Christ,
may your love bring light.

Where disaster has brought devastation,
flood, famine, volcano, earthquake or storm shattering lives,
Lord Jesus Christ,
may your love bring light.

Where hearts are closed to you and others,
doubt, fear, dogma and prejudice creating alienation,
Lord Jesus Christ,
may your love bring light.

Come to our world, Lord, and heal its wounds,
shining in the darkness
and restoring joy, faith, hope and love.
Lord Jesus Christ,
may your love bring light.
Amen.

287
Lord Jesus Christ,
come as light into our world,
bringing food where there is hunger,
peace where there is war
and justice where there is exploitation.
Gracious Lord,
shine upon us.

Come as light into our lives,
bringing happiness in our homes,
joy in our relationships
and contentment in our work and leisure.
Gracious Lord,
shine upon us.

Come as light into our darkness,
bringing love instead of hatred,
good instead of evil
and hope instead of despair.
Gracious Lord,
shine upon us.

Come as light into our souls,
bringing faith instead of doubt,
fulfilment instead of emptiness
and life instead of death.
Gracious Lord,
shine upon us.

Come, Lord Jesus,
and shine in the hearts of all.
Amen.

288

Lord Jesus Christ,
there's nothing special about us,
nothing exceptional that will make people sit up and take notice.
We're not particularly good or loving,
much though we'd like to be,
nor do we possess saintly or special qualities.
We're just ordinary people seeking to love and serve you better.
Yet, with your help,
we can make a difference nonetheless.
In various ways,
no matter how small,
we can help to brighten up this world.
Shine upon us,
so that our light in turn may shine among others.
Show us what you would have us do,
and help us to do it.
Amen.

289

Bring light, Lord, into our troubled world,
and shine in every place and experience of darkness.
Disperse the shadows of disease and disaster,
sickness and suffering,
hardship and hunger,
war and terror –
everything that destroys and divides,
alienating people from themselves, one another and you.
In Christ's name we pray.
Amen.

290

Come, Lord, into the darkness of our world,
the shadow of sorrow,
suffering,
hunger,
despair,
hatred,
evil
and death.
Bring a new dawn,
new beginnings,
the light of your love shining on all.
Amen.

291

Lord Jesus Christ,
in a world where so much holds people captive,
denying the life and light you long to give them,
bring an end to the darkness.
Comfort those who grieve,
support those who suffer,
provide for those in need,
and strengthen the weak in body, mind or spirit.
Encourage all who work to disperse the gloom,
and inspire us and others to respond in turn,
so that there may be laughter after tears,
delight after despair,
and sunshine after shadow.
Amen.

292

Lord Jesus Christ,
light of the world,
shine again upon us we pray,
and illuminate the darkness of this world
through your life-giving grace.
Amen.

293

Lord Jesus Christ,
may the flame of faith burn brightly within us,
and your light shine in our hearts,
so that we, in turn, may bring light to others,
to the glory of your name.
Amen.

294

Reach out, Lord, into our world,
and cause your light to shine.
Where hatred brings war,
disaster causes devastation,
injustice leads to poverty,
intolerance breeds violence,
disease creates despair
and life entails suffering,
be there in the darkness,
restoring joy, faith, hope and love.
Amen.

295
Thank you, Lord, for being with us in our darkness,
your light continuing to shine through trouble and tragedy,
turmoil and tears.
Break through where shadows still linger,
into our doubt and disbelief,
our disobedience,
our flawed commitment and weakness of will.
Illuminate all through the radiance of your love.
Amen.

296
Light of the world,
shine wherever there is darkness today.
Where there is pain and sorrow,
may the brilliance of your love bring joy.
Where there is sickness and suffering,
may your healing touch bring sunshine after the storm.
Where there is greed and corruption,
may your radiance scatter the shadows.
Where there is hatred and bitterness,
may your brightness dispel the clouds.
Amen.

297
Shine afresh into the darkness of this world, Lord,
and disperse the shadows of sorrow,
hurt,
hatred,
violence
and war.
Break into the night-time of evil and injustice,
and usher in a new dawn.
Illuminate all in the sunshine of your love.
Amen.

298
Lord Jesus Christ,
shine afresh into our hearts,
so that even where all seems bleak we may find reason to celebrate,
cause to rejoice.
Come into the darkness of our world,
its hatred, suffering and evil,
and somehow, through your grace,
work within such things for good.
Amen.

Reflective prayer

299
Lord,
there is so much I don't understand,
so much that, if I'm honest, troubles me:
questions concerning evil and suffering,
the nature of truth and authority of Scripture;
uncertainties concerning the origins of life and our ultimate goal;
doubts over matters of creed and doctrine,
even sometimes your very existence.
I'm don't question lightly, far from it,
for such things strike at the heart of my faith,
threatening everything I believe –
or, at least, everything I'm meant to believe –
yet I can't help it,
for there's no use pretending,
no point claiming everything is all right when it clearly isn't.
I might fool others,
but not you,
or me,
so where would that get us?
No,
I can only continue searching,
looking for answers for as long as it takes,
trusting that one day, in your own time,
the quest will be over,
the journey complete,
the understanding I seek finally granted.

Until then, Lord,
go with me,
lead me,
teach me.
Show me, as you have promised, that those who seek *will* find!
Amen.

Closing prayers

300
Light of life,
shine upon us.
Light of truth,
shine within us.
Light of love,
shine from us.
Light of the world,
shine through us.
Lord Jesus Christ,
wherever there is darkness
shine your light,
and may it never be extinguished.
Amen.

301
As light filled the sky for the shepherds,
so, gracious God, may your glory shine in our hearts.
As a star guided wise men from the East,
so may your love guide our footsteps.
As John the Baptist witnessed to the light,
so may we bring light in turn to others.
As you came through your Son, shining in the darkness,
so be with us even in life's bleakest moments.
In your grace and mercy,
may Christ, the light of the world,
be *our* light,
our life,
now, and for evermore.
Amen.

302

Go on your way,
light shining upon you,
pulsating within you
and shining from you,
through Jesus Christ our Lord.
Amen.

303

Whether life brings light or darkness,
joy or sorrow,
pleasure or pain,
satisfaction or disappointment,
be with us, Lord,
your love shining over us though we may not see it,
and lead us safely onwards
until we find our final fulfilment in you.
Amen.

304

Lord Jesus Christ,
so work within us that we may not simply talk of light
but also bring it to others,
your love shining out through our life and witness,
your goodness reflected in who we are and what we do.
Amen.

305

Lord Jesus Christ,
whatever the future may hold,
wherever life may lead,
go with us,
scattering the clouds
and bringing sunshine into our lives.
Fill us with light and life,
today and always.
Amen.

Index